The First

State University

A Walking Guide

by Marguerite Schumann

Revised Edition

The University of North Carolina Press

Chapel Hill and London

© 1972, 1985 The University of

North Carolina Press

Manufactured in the United States of America

Library of Congress Cataloging in Publication Data

Schumann, Marguerite E.

The first state university.

1. University of North Carolina (Chapel Hill campus)—
Guide-books. I. Title.
LD3944.S38   1985   378.756′565   84-26957
ISBN 0-8078-4130-7

Contents

Phillips Hall 90
Peabody Hall 91
Carolina Inn 92

Walk 5: Starting at Brooks Hall; ending at Mitchell Hall

Brooks Hall 95
Battle Park 96
Forest Theatre 97
Paul Green Theatre 98
Old Chapel Hill Cemetery 99
Institute of Government
(Knapp Building) 100
William Donald Carmichael
Auditorium 101
Woollen Gymnasium 101
Robert Allison Fetzer
Gymnasium 102
Morehead-Patterson Memorial
Tower 103
Kenan Memorial Stadium 104
William C. Coker Hall 105
Wilson Hall 105
Elisha Mitchell Hall 106

Walk 6: Starting at Beard Hall; ending at North Carolina Memorial Hospital

Beard Hall 109
Carrington Hall 109
Berryhill Hall (Basic Medical
Science) 110
Brinkhous-Bullitt Preclinical
Education Building 111
Rosenau Hall 112
Health Sciences Library 112
MacNider Hall 113
Brauer Hall (Dental Education
Building) 114
Burnett-Womack Clinical Sciences
Building 114
North Carolina Memorial
Hospital 115

Accessible by car

Student Activities Center 116
William Rand Kenan, Jr., Center of
North Carolina 117
North Carolina Botanical
Garden 118

A walk in Chapel Hill

The rediscovery of walking may be among the happiest contributions of America's Age of Ecology. Walking, a gently tiring, total experience of mind and muscle, allows the unhurried sight of things and the savoring of their accompanying sounds and smells.

The walker in Chapel Hill is placed in a particularly intimate relationship with the good life.

First, it is a town with a university campus at its heart. *The New Yorker* magazine once provided this description: "A campus is unique. It is above and beyond government. It is on the highest plane of life. Those who live there know the smell of good air, and they always take pains to spell truth with a small 't.' This is its secret strength and its contribution to the web of freedom: this is why the reading room of a college library is the very temple of democracy."*

Second, Chapel Hill has one of the most beautiful campuses in the nation. Men with a strong sense of esthetics have lived on this land, thought about it, and shaped it for nineteen decades. They began with the undisturbed forest, they cut the campus and village out of the forest, and the primeval richness of the forest still dominates. Thomas Wolfe, one of the University's most famous sons, wrote of its "century-long struggle in the forest," of its remoteness and isolated

charm, and the "rare romantic quality of the atmosphere."

On the land that has been taken from the forest, the gardeners, amateur and professional, have created an uncommon architecture of grasses, plants, and trees. In Chapel Hill more than 160 species of vegetation from mountains and coastal areas meet and flourish, and with them has been created an extraordinary garden town.

The singular beauty of Chapel Hill can be traced to four men who established a standard that others followed.

David Lowry Swain, third president of the University (1835–68), expressed the wish for a botanical garden as early as 1844; in 1848 he employed the first English-trained gardener to supervise the annual planting of $1,000 worth of ornamental trees and shrubs. A landscape plan of the campus which Swain commissioned from A. J. Davis in the mid-nineteenth century is now preserved in the Metropolitan Museum of Art in New York.

Elisha Mitchell, professor from 1818 to 1857, served more than a dozen academic and administrative functions, among them being superintendent of buildings and grounds. He directed crews of slaves who built the first fences of gray volcanic rock around the campus in 1838 to keep the stray village livestock off the University grounds. Reminiscent of the walls in Mitchell's native Connecticut, the fences were copied by private property owners in the village and

*Reprinted by permission of New Yorker Magazine, Inc.

still are an integral part of the look of Chapel Hill. A more impressive monument to Mitchell is Mount Mitchell in the Black Mountains of the Blue Ridge chain, which at 6,684 feet is the highest peak east of the Rockies. The professor fell to his death there while attempting to verify the mountain's elevation, which had been disputed.

Kemp Plummer Battle, fifth president from 1876 to 1891, created the paths and bridges in Battle Park and by 1889 had restored the campus to its pre–Civil War beauty. While the town had not been touched by armed conflict, four thousand horses and men had been quartered from what is now Tenney Circle up Rosemary Street to the former Town Hall, as well as on the campus. The years of Reconstruction had been marked by vandalism and neglect as well.

William Chambers Coker, professor of botany from 1902 to 1945, built the Coker Arboretum and supervised the landscape architecture of the campus for many years.

Others have cared about the beauty of the campus over the decades and have added to it in their own ways. There are still evidences of plants that came to Chapel Hill in 1857 after Commodore Perry's expedition to open Japan to the Western world. Although most of the specimens brought back to the United States were destined for official national collections, alumnus James Dobbins, Secretary of the Navy, saw to it that some, like the red spider lilies that form an autumn glory in the Arboretum, came to Chapel Hill. Seven decades later alumni from Washington, D.C., sent the Japanese cherry trees that now edge McCorkle Place with pink during the spring. Pocket-sized gardens here and there on the campus are the work of other alumni who cared.

Walking in Chapel Hill is also an experience of the mind because of the importance of the University of North Carolina in American history. The campus site was selected—the hill of the Chapel of New Hope—because the "big roads" of the state crossed here during the eighteenth century. In a symbolic sense, the big roads still lead to Chapel Hill, for this is the "capitol of the Southern mind" (Mark Ethridge) and "a holy hill" (Frank Porter Graham).

This was the first state university to open its classroom doors, and its first building, Old East, has been designated as a National Historic Landmark. The University established the first astronomical observatory connected with an American university, and its planetarium, the first owned by a university, has contributed to the training of the first American astronauts to penetrate space and walk on the moon.

The physical campus serves as an intellectual Westminster Abbey for North Carolina; while its great men are not physically buried here, their lives and deeds are enshrined here, and the University buildings bearing their surnames are a part of the daily vocabulary.

Here in the buildings are represented the union of a remarkable group of men whose biographies furnish an intellectual and social history of North Carolina. They range from Revolutionary and Civil War patriots to twentieth-century industrialists, from Ku Klux Klan leaders to international statesmen, from eccentrics and rogues to a president of the United States. Here are memorialized men who edited regional newspapers, who wrote nationally acclaimed novels, who dreamed of social reform, and who taught the youth of North Carolina over nearly two centuries. Thirty of the names now chiseled in stone or cast in metal on building facades are those who gave much of their working lives to Carolina.

The building faces illustrate the changing tastes that have occurred in architectural style since our nation was young. While UNC is a campus that has been planned from the beginning, it has also been replanned several times, just as a shell must change to accommodate a growing organism inside. To detail the metamorphoses of facade and function for each building lies beyond the limitations of this guide; such details are given for the historic buildings predating the Civil War, and a few others.

The thing that makes Chapel Hill different is that it is a very old university and that it is set in the South. It has endured. It has suffered vicissitudes in its founding and in its middle years. In the twentieth century it has come to greatness. At the same time it has mellowed into charm. The years look down from its venerable walls onto a well-planted, well-tended campus garden that is renewed with each changing season and each successive generation.

Walk now on the campus of the first state university and discover its past and present delights for yourself.

Marguerite Schumann

Acknowledgments

The author is deeply indebted to William S. Powell, author of *The First State University: A Pictorial History of the University of North Carolina* and professor of history at the University, for his personal and professional encouragement and for his advice concerning historical photographs for this edition. Although many historical materials were consulted in preparing this guide, primary dependence was placed on Kemp P. Battle's two-volume *History of the University of North Carolina* and Archibald Henderson's *The Campus of the First State University*. Rachael Long of the University Planning Office has been helpful in furnishing dates and other information about recent campus buildings.

Jane Hamborsky, of the University of North Carolina PhotoLab, a division of the Media and Instructional Support Center, was a great help in securing the photographs for this edition. New photographs were made of all the buildings and points of interest on the tours to reflect the changes that have taken place on the campus since the first edition was published. Jerry Cotten, photographic archivist with the North Carolina Collection at Wilson Library, made suggestions and located negatives for the historical photographs.

How to use the walking guide

This tour guide, covering seventy-six buildings and thirteen other spots of interest in the main section of the University campus and the nearest residential area of Chapel Hill, will prove an ideal companion to the walker who wishes to acquaint himself with the history of the University and the men behind that history. The geographical area has been limited to easy, one-hour walks in the vicinity of McCorkle Place and Polk Place, the heart of the old campus, and some sections of the South Campus. The last several points of interest are spread geographically and are most easily toured by car. Divided into six walks, each with an accompanying map of the route, the buildings are described both pictorially and with text. The basic facts of the history and function of each building begin each entry; the material that follows may be saved for later reading at home, as it includes anecdotes concerning life within the building or interesting bits of information concerning the individual for whom the building was named.

Limitations were placed on the length of each entry so that the volume could be kept to a small, convenient format, enabling the walker to easily read while walking and viewing each building or point of interest. The reader who wishes to learn more about the University and its campus should consult *The First State University: A Pictorial History of the University of North Carolina* by William S. Powell. It contains many rare pictures of the eighteenth- and nineteenth-century campus, along with explanatory captions and concise essays, in addition to ample coverage of the University today.

WALK 1

Starting at Old East;
ending at Davie Hall

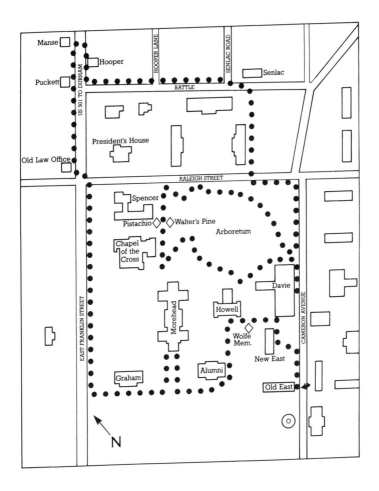

Old East

1793, lengthened and third story added 1824, remodeled 1848, interior rebuilt 1924

Old East, the oldest state university building in the nation and a dormitory throughout those years, was designated a National Historic Landmark in 1966 for possessing "exceptional value in commemorating the history of the United States." It is identified as such by a bronze plaque on its southeast corner. The building was designed to face east "just as the capitols at Washington and Raleigh faced under the influence of Orientalization."

Because of complaints such as those from the "Father of the University," William Richardson Davie, who declared that the building was "infamously done" by a "mechanic" of Chatham County, it was given a face-lifting by the eminent New York architect Alexander Jackson Davis in 1824. Davis provided the series of tall exterior piers on the north, which one critic described as "conspicuously Egyptian in character" while another likened them to "Greek antae."

The state constitution of 1776 provided for the founding of a university. The charter was ratified by the General Assembly in 1789. The cornerstone for Old East was laid on 12 October 1793; nearly a century later that date was officially declared University Day.

General William Richardson Davie, Revolutionary patriot, governor of North Carolina, and recipient of the University's first honorary doctor of laws degree, laid the cornerstone. He had sponsored and steered the bill that created the University, had prepared the ordinance fixing the seat of the University, and played a central part in the construction of buildings and selection of the faculty.

His duties were remarkably diverse: he contracted for the design of the University bookplate; he was responsible for having the avenue cleared, grubbed, and put in order; and he saw to having the spring cleaned.

Davie was a high official in the Masonic order and he was dressed in his lodge regalia as he marched

3

in military tread to the cornerstone ceremony, accompanied by Masons from Hillsborough and Raleigh. At the site the members formed a double line for state dignitaries to pass through. During the University's early years all cornerstones were laid in Masonic ceremonies.

Sealed into the cornerstone that day by Davie's silver trowel was a commemorative plate reading, "The Right Worshipfull William Richardson Davie, Grand Master of the most Ancient and Honorable Fraternity of Freemasons in the State of North Carolina, one of the trustees of the University of the said state . . . assisted by the other commissioners and the Brethren of the Eagle and Independence Lodges, on the 12th day of October in the Year of Masonry 5793 and in the 18th year of the American Independence laid the cornerstone of this edifice."

The cornerstone was vandalized sometime between 1865 and 1875 and the commemorative plate was stolen. In 1916 it was discovered in a pile of scrap brass destined for melting at a foundry in Tennessee. The foundry's owner, who was an alumnus of UNC, recognizing the name Davie, had the plate cleaned and returned to its rightful place. The plate may be seen in the North Carolina Collection of the Louis Round Wilson Library.

On 15 January 1795, Governor Richard Dobbs Spaight drove from Raleigh over twenty-eight miles of red mud and jagged rocks for the official opening of the University's doors and sent out word that "youth disposed to enter the University could come forward with the assurance of being received." Hinton James was so disposed and entered as the first student on 12 February.

Both the residential and instructional life of the University centered in Old East for twenty years. Within a short time the crowding in the building became intolerable. Fifty-six students were squeezed into fourteen one-window rooms. To get

OLD EAST
THE OLDEST STATE UNIVERSITY BUILDING
IN THE NATION
CORNERSTONE LAID BY
WILLIAM RICHARDSON DAVIE
OCTOBER 12, 1793
THIRD STORY, 1822 · NORTH ADDITION, 1844
DESIGNED BY ALEXANDER JACKSON DAVIS

away from their fellowmen the students erected huts in the forest and in the unfinished shell of South Building. When the weather was too bad for students to study in their huts, this was considered a valid excuse for unprepared lessons.

Student life sheltered within the walls of Old East was boisterous and occasionally violent, partly because of the time in history, but also because of the rigid University rules, the few vacation periods, and the lack of organized physical activity.

There were, of course, the classic student pranks of throwing frogs and terrapins into the Frenchmaster's room and carrying off carriages and gates. But in addition there were reports of gun fire, kegs of whiskey in student rooms, stabbings with pen knives, breaking tutors' doors and threatening them with violence, torturing animals with flaming turpentine, and plotting mischief further afield—attempting arson on a trustee's house,

cutting the corn in a villager's field, and stealing beehives.

In 1799 there was a rebellion in which the principal was beaten. Shortly after the turn of the century came the Great Secession, in which forty-five students remonstrated with the faculty over the severity of new regulations. As a result of the altercation, forty-one students seceded and went home, including a large majority of the ablest and most mature students who later attained prominence in public office as governor, judge, state senator, speaker of the house, and members of the general assembly.

There were intermittent episodes of dueling and resultant expulsions, but no deaths by violence are recorded. There are frequent reports like the following from President Battle: "he lost his diploma for striking down Haywood with a club in consequence of words spoken at a convivial banquet," and "six pistols and two dirks appeared at Washington's birthday dinner in 1816." Only one alumnus is known to have

died on the gallows, and this was for the slaying of his sister shortly after he had been expelled from the University. His campus crime was a drinking and card-playing frolic in his room, which was followed up on Sunday (when he should have been repenting his Saturday sins) by illuminating his windows with numerous candles.

The trustees of the University were much concerned with student conduct and interfered regularly in these matters. Consequently it was ironic that Davie's oldest son pulled a knife on another student at a commencement ball because of a tripping and foot-trampling incident.

New East

1859, remodeled 1926, 1969

A pair of Italianate buildings, New East and New West, appeared on the campus when enrollment had more than doubled in the decade following the Gold Rush. They provided student rooms and permanent homes for the literary societies, which virtually controlled student activities through the nineteenth century. The Philanthropic Society Assembly Hall is on the fourth floor of New East. The rest of the building is now occupied by the Department of City and Regional Planning.

Central heating was introduced to the University in New East and New West, but the furnace and hot water system was not a success. Notice the Italian architectural characteristics: heavy brackets supporting wide overhanging eaves and the central pavilion flanked by wings.

During Reconstruction (1865–76), the literary society halls were pillaged by citizens as well as occupying troops. Professor David Patrick looted the Phi society hall, carrying off a velvet rug, some carpet, and handsome chairs in order to entertain trustees at the president's house, contending that a communistic spirit prevailed after the closing of the University and that its property belonged to the people.

Membership in the literary societies was determined by geography. Students from the eastern half of the state joined the Phi society (which they pronounced Phi-lan-thropic rather than Phil-an-thropic); those from the west joined the Dialectic.

Wolfe Memorial

An 850-pound bronze relief sculpture of an angel mounted on a concrete slab stands at the northeast corner of New East to mark the association of Thomas Wolfe, the unbroken colt of American letters, with the University of North Carolina from which he graduated in 1920. Wolfe studied playwrighting in New East.

The marker is inscribed with a familiar line from *Look Homeward, Angel*: "O lost, and by the wind grieved, ghost, come back again." The memorial is the gift of the class of 1966 and was designed by Richard W. Kinnaird of the UNC Department of Art.

The Wolfe Memorial stands at the edge of a courtyard planted with azaleas in memory of Sara Lee Gifford, former student in the School of Journalism.

Wolfe wrote for the Playmakers (taking the title role in his play, The Return of Buck Gavin) and edited the campus newspaper. On one occasion, after he had printed a photo of a coed embracing a man, her father rushed in, threatening to sue. "You can't sue me," Wolfe said. "And why can't I?" the irate parent inquired. Wolfe rose to his 6½-foot height with the words "Because, sir, I am a minor."

Wolfe's thinly disguised descriptions of "Pulpit Hill" and vignettes of faculty figures have shaped a monument for UNC in every library of the literate world. "The wilderness crept up to it like a beast," he wrote of Pulpit/Chapel Hill.

Howell Hall

1906

Now the School of Journalism, this structure was built as Chemistry Hall and later used for pharmacy. It commemorates the pharmacy school's founder and dean for thirty-three years, Edward Vernon Howell, who was called "the most distinctive personality Chapel Hill has ever known." After two short-lived attempts by the University to create a pharmacy department, Howell was persuaded in 1896 to leave his retail drug business in Rocky Mount to begin work with seventeen students in a single lecture room, with a yearly budget for library books and periodicals of $3.00 and a salary of $25.00 per month, plus a small commission for every student.

At that time anyone at UNC was eligible to play football, from president to janitor, and Howell starred for an undefeated eleven, making a fifty-five yard run, despite a broken finger and nose, to defeat Virginia 6-2 in the key game of 1898.

His housekeeping was that of a traditionally careless bachelor. "At one end of his rare old mahogany dining room table would be a dish or plate, and the rest of the surface would be covered by a jumble of manuscripts, books, and newspaper clippings," Dean J. G. Beard of the School of Pharmacy later recalled. Long after his death, some of this magpie collection, about 1600 items, was given to the Southern Historical Collection by James K. Kyser and Emily Royster Howell Kyser. The collection contained historical materials concerning North Carolina from 1725 to 1871. Howell owned the first automobile in Chapel Hill.

Alumni Building

1898

For more than forty years—through Civil War, Reconstruction, and beyond—no new building appeared on the campus. Alumni Building, built largely by subscription within that group, was the first new construction after New East and New West were built in 1859. Described as "a scaled-down model of the New York Public Library," it today houses anthropology, archaeology, and the African and Afro-American Studies Curriculum. The Research Laboratories of Anthropology, which has a collection of more than one million specimens, displays (in the ground-floor corridor) a group of projectile points dating from 10,000 B.C., burial urns, pottery, skulls, and ornaments.

The alumni body represented by this building had played a commanding role in the political life of the state and nation during the nineteenth century. National officials had included President James K. Polk; Vice President William Rufus King; two presiding officers of the U.S. Senate; a speaker of the House of Representatives; four secretaries of the navy; secretaries of state, war, and the interior; a postmaster general; an attorney general; and a solicitor general.

Morehead Building and Planetarium

1949, 1973

The John Motley Morehead Foundation was created in 1945, and four years later the Morehead Building was presented to the University. Within the original building, which is designed in the Monticello tradition, are the Morehead Planetarium, the Copernican Orrery, the Genevieve B. Morehead Art Gallery, the State Dining Room, and several lounges. This was the first planetarium to be owned by an American university.

In the planetarium, the first production model VI Carl Zeiss projector and adjuncts (now automated), installed in 1969 as a replacement for the original instrument which came from Sweden, projects celestial bodies and their movements on the sixty-eight-foot hemispherical steel dome. The instrument is the sixth Zeiss projector to be installed in the United States and the first major installation on a college campus. Regular planetarium programs are presented for tens of thousands of school children and general audiences each year, with the most popular offering occurring at Christmas. Between 1960 and 1975, forty-three American astronauts were trained here in celestial navigation.

The thirty-five-foot, walk-in model Copernican Orrery is one of two in the world, demonstrating how planets revolve around the sun while rotating on their own axes and the "moons" revolve around the planets.

In the walnut-paneled rotunda, flanking a portrait of Mrs. Morehead, is a distinguished collection of seventeenth- and eighteenth-century painting, including works by Rembrandt, Anthony Van Dyck, Thomas Gainsborough, Henry Raeburn, Rembrandt Peale, and others. Also in the room is a large aneroid barometer by Henry Brown and Son and a great clock, with a fourteen-foot pendulum, by Howard. A different English cathedral peal is heard each day of the week.

Exhibit space for changing art shows and a scale model of the

University campus adjoin the rotunda, and science exhibits are found in the basement.

A 1973 addition to the building, doubling its size, contains a twenty-four-inch Cassegrain reflector telescope, a ballroom, and the office of the Morehead Foundation Scholarship Program. At any time, there are about 250 undergraduates holding Morehead Scholarships, patterned after Oxford's prestigious Rhodes awards. About one-third of the Morehead Scholars are women and about 10 percent are black. The Morehead hybrid-rose garden and sundial, one of the largest of its type with a diameter of thirty-five feet, are north of the building.

"John Motley Morehead has become for North Carolina what the Medici and Borgias once were to Renaissance Florence—a patron of culture and enlightenment with few peers," an editorial in the Greensboro Daily News once stated. In the first quarter-century of the foundation's existence more than $30 million was given to the University for scholarships and other purposes.

Morehead was the eleventh member of his family to graduate from UNC, and the third to bear the given names John Motley. The first, his grandfather, who was twice governor of North Carolina, took as his primary goals the providing of educational opportunities for children and the construction of an east-west railroad across the state.

"Uncle Mot," as he was known to many of the 425 Morehead scholars whom he had met personally before his death in 1965, made his most important scientific discovery less than a year after he graduated from UNC in 1891. While working as a chemical engineer for his father in Spray, N.C., trying to make aluminum in the world's first electric arc furnace, Morehead discovered calcium carbide and perfected the present-day process for its economic manufacture.

"We just got a lump of this stuff about the size of a coconut," Morehead said in a campus interview shortly before his death. "I took it back to the laboratory to analyze it. When we put it in water it gave off clouds of gas, and when we lit the gas it burned with clouds of smoke. Well, I didn't have any gas analyzing apparatus up there, so I sent a piece of the stuff down here to Dr. Venable, who said it was acetylene gas."

From this discovery grew the Union Carbide Corporation, which at the time of Morehead's death had seventy-three thousand employees scattered throughout the world and produced more than six hundred products.

Morehead was identified with the oxygen-acetylene gas industry as a designing electro-chemical engineer all his life. In 1899 he designed an apparatus for analyzing gases that became standard equipment in industrial laboratories, schools, and colleges. He held many patents for improvements in the electric arc furnace and other electro-chemical processes, and he was the author of The Analysis of Industrial Gases.

After 1917 he lived in New York, where Union Carbide had its headquarters, and he served as mayor of Rye from 1925 to 1930. One of his last direct benefactions was a new city hall of Federal design, which he provided for Rye when the town was contemplating a low-cost contemporary building.

By President Herbert Hoover's appointment, he was envoy-extraordinary and minister plenipotentiary to Sweden in the early 1930s, and during that time was the only foreigner honored with the gold medal Kungl. Svenska Vetenskopsakademien. He received honorary degrees from the University of North Carolina, Wake Forest, Davidson, and Upsala University.

Throughout his life Morehead was fascinated with clocks. In addition to the clock in the rotunda, he

13

placed another important clock in the town of Rye, N.Y. It pleased him to wear his own Swiss custom-made watch on a shoestring.

The Morehead-Patterson Memorial Bell Tower on south campus is another evidence of Morehead's across-the-board benefactions to his alma mater.

Graham Memorial Building

1931

Home of the Department of Dramatic Art, the PlayMakers Repertory Company, and the Institute of Outdoor Drama, this building was originally designed as a student union. It memorializes Edward Kidder Graham, ninth president of the University (1914–18), who died in the influenza epidemic of World War I. The original Carolina Playmakers, founded in 1918, achieved national reputation for promoting native playwrighting, originating outdoor drama that began with Paul Green's *The Lost Colony* on Roanoke Island in 1937, and for alumni in the performing arts. The Play-Makers Repertory Company was founded in its present form in 1976. The Institute of Outdoor Drama was founded in 1963 as a central agency for such activities throughout the country. The McKenzie Doll Collection of International Dress, more than six hundred items, is located in the basement lobby.

It is said that in Graham's brief tenure he transformed the oldest state university into the newest state university. He formulated a North Carolina plan in which the "university was an instrument of democracy for realizing all the high and healthful aspirations of the state."

Graham convinced the North Carolina legislature that their University should receive their support. In 1917, for the first time in history, the legislature granted the president's budget request in full. Previously, 75 percent of the campus buildings had been private gifts.

Chapel of the Cross (Episcopal)

1843, second structure 1924

This parish was organized as the Church of the Atonement on 13 May 1842 by the Reverend William Mercer Green. Services were held in his parlor. The next year construction, employing slave labor, began on a small brick Gothic Revival structure designed by Thomas U. Walter of Philadelphia. It was consecrated 19 October 1848 as the Chapel of the Cross. Additions were made in 1891 and 1917 and restorations in 1950, 1961, and 1980. Notice the slave gallery, supported by wooden pillars. A new church and parish hall, connected to the original by a cloister, was built of pink Mount Airy granite during 1924–25 by Durham industrialist William A. Erwin in memory of his grandfather, Dr. William R. Holt.

The Reverend Mr. Green was graduated from UNC in 1818 with President Polk. He was chaplain of the University and professor of belles lettres from 1839 to 1849. Green established a brickyard in order to build the church; he also contracted to furnish bricks for University buildings, among them the Playmakers Theatre. In respect for the Sabbath, Green had the brickyard fires extinguished at midnight each Saturday. Crumbling masses of half-baked bricks resulted. He was bishop of Mississippi from 1850 to 1887 and, during part of that time (1866–78), was chancellor of the University of the South at Sewanee, Tennessee.

A second bishop came from the parish. The Rt. Reverend Peter James Lee was consecrated a bishop of Virginia on 19 May 1984.

In the small chapel in 1977 the Reverend Pauli Murray celebrated her first eucharist after ordination as a priest. She was among the first small group of women ordained with church approval and was the first black woman in that role. The Reverend Miss Murray's grandmother had been baptized in the chapel as a slave baby in 1854.

Spencer Hall

1924

Spencer Hall, named for Cornelia Phillips Spencer, is a stately Georgian women's dormitory in a handsome setting and has large, graciously furnished public rooms. In the parlor are a collection of oil paintings of historic places and personages including two portraits of Mrs. Spencer, and a square rosewood piano dated 1868. This hall was the first built for women at UNC and was named for the first woman to be given a doctor of laws degree from any Southern institution. A dormitory at UNC–Greensboro is also named for her.

Mrs. Spencer, poet, social historian, and journalist, was described by Governor Zebulon Vance as "the smartest woman in North Carolina—and the smartest man, too." Mrs. Spencer was a self-appointed press agent for the cause of reopening the University after the Civil War. On her birthday, 20 March 1875, when she received word that her objective had been accomplished, she gathered children and friends, climbed to the attic of South Building, and rang the bell. This story, retold by her grandnephew Phillips Russell, won the distinguished Mayflower Award for writing. After living in Chapel Hill for sixty-nine years, Mrs. Spencer died in Cambridge, Mass., holding a picture of the UNC campus in her hands. A World War II Liberty Ship that was named for her was sunk by enemy action in October 1943.

President's House

402 East Franklin Street   1907

This spacious residence, one of sixteen campus buildings to appear during President Venable's administration, stands at the high point of a three-quarters acre lot on the eastern edge of the campus. Its portico has Corinthian columns, and there are porches on three sides supported by Ionic pillars. The original cost was $15,000; its remodeling in 1929 involved nearly $7,000.

The first house on this site, built early in the nineteenth century by Helen Hogg Hooper, became the president's home when she and President Caldwell were married and he moved into the residence. Mrs. Caldwell set considerable style in the house. Here is one of her party menus: roast turkey and duck, roast and boiled beef, boiled chicken, Irish and sweet potatoes, turnips, rice, carrots, parsnips, cabbage, stewed apples, boiled pudding, baked potato pudding, damson tarts, currant tarts, apple pies, and whips.

The house was occupied by President Swain from 1849 to 1868, and in its parlor took place Chapel Hill's best known romance—that of Eleanor Swain and Union General Smith B. Atkins. The reception following the unpopular marriage was harassed by students who tolled the South Building bell for three hours.

Three presidents of the United States—Polk, Buchanan, and Andrew Johnson—were received at the Swain home. Buchanan was feted at an open air dinner beneath the oak trees. This house burned on Christmas morning 1886.

Old Law Office

401 East Franklin Street

1840s, remodeled 1983

The beginnings of the UNC Law School were made in this Italian-style cottage (also called the Stone or Stucco Cottage) when Judge William Horn Battle read law privately with students between 1845 and 1868 and again from 1877 to 1879. The cottage, the first law office in Chapel Hill, was built by Battle's law partner Samuel Field Phillips, who after the Civil War was appointed solicitor general of the United States by Ulysses S. Grant, an appointment that gave great offense to the citizens of Chapel Hill. "Mr. Sam" assisted Battle in law instruction for some years and during 1847 ran a preparatory school for boys in his portion of the office. The small building is now a private residence.

Judge Battle, who served on the state supreme court, 1852–68, was a UNC graduate in 1820, a trustee for thirty-eight years, and a trusted adviser to two UNC presidents. For twenty-five years he counseled President David Swain on the problems of University government, and for the last years of his life filled the same function for his son, President Kemp P. Battle.

Battle, an abstemious man, was concerned when his doctor prescribed a hot toddy before breakfast. One morning while dressing Battle said to his wife, "I will not take another toddy!" "Why not?" she asked. "I think it is doing you good." "Well, I think so too," he replied, "but I found myself dressing fast in order to get it. Don't make me another."

Widow Puckett House

501 East Franklin Street   Between 1817 and 1820

This private house was built for Postmaster John Puckett, an early resident of the village. It was once thought to be the oldest house in Chapel Hill because there is evidence in letters that students boarded at Puckett's as early as 1795 in preference to Steward's Hall on the campus, but this took place in an earlier structure.

In 1826 it became the home of Dr. James Phillips, who for forty-one years was professor of mathematics and natural philosophy. Here his children grew up: Cornelia Phillips Spencer, author and social historian; Dr. Charles Phillips, who later took over his father's professorship; and Samuel Field Phillips, for twelve years solicitor general of the United States.

When Union troops occupied Chapel Hill, the Phillips men thought the best place to hide their watches was inside the dust-covered Caldwell telescope. They underestimated the keen eyes of the soldiers, however. When the commanding officer heard of the theft, he ordered the watches returned.

Freshmen were told that Phillips was a reformed pirate and an expert with sword and stick. Actually, his most colorful youthful experience in England was seeing Napoleon pacing the deck of the Bellerophon. Phillips died at morning prayers in Gerrard Hall, with textbooks and classroom keys in hand.

Presbyterian Manse

513 East Franklin Street   Around 1865

Dr. Charles Phillips, chairman of the faculty, moved into this private house when the University reopened in 1875. He had been at UNC twenty-two years when he was among those cast adrift after the Civil War. After a number of years on the faculty of Davidson College, Phillips was brought home to his old position when the University was reorganized.

Like his father, Charles Phillips was both a mathematician and a Presbyterian minister. He led the chapel music with a tuning fork and a carrying voice. Even at the funeral of Phillips' oldest son, the presiding minister said, "It is painful for me to call on the parent of the deceased to raise the tune, but there is no other course to pursue."

Phillips was a large (230 pounds), brilliant, impulsive man. A visiting college president once said, "Where have you been hiding this man Phillips? Why, sir, he has a brain as big as his abdomen." He took little care of his health. He rose from a hasty dinner on a blistering day to lead his class on a twenty-two-mile hike to University Station and back. He stayed up all night, after a full week of commencement activities, to prepare a summary of events for the press. After a drenching in the winter rain while burying a member of his church, he taught for an hour in wet clothes. He became afflicted with gout and only four years after returning to Chapel Hill was obliged to retire.

Hooper House

504 East Franklin Street   1814

William Hooper, grandson and namesake of one of North Carolina's signers of the Declaration of Independence, built this private home early in his career as a member of the faculty. He served UNC from 1810 to 1837, with the exception of several years at Princeton. Notice the end chimneys that stand free of the house above the second floor, and the general simplicity of design.

After leaving Chapel Hill, Hooper had frequent "impairments of health" that caused him to change residence and employment. He had earlier given up the Episcopal priesthood because he had been "cursed by a precocious two-year-old to whom he was administering the sacrament of baptism." This led to a thoughtful reexamination of his theological position, and in 1831 he became a Baptist.

Hooper wrote a report to the Baptist State Convention that led to the establishment of Wake Forest College, where he later became president. His resignation from the presidency of Chowan Female Institute came about when he, a disapprover of secession, refused to allow his girls to hoist a Confederate flag. Hooper's life ended on a note of happy historical significance; he died six weeks after celebrating the centennial of the Declaration of Independence in Philadelphia, where he had been invited as a lineal descendent of one of the signers.

Senlac

203 Battle Lane   1843

Senlac, now the Baptist Campus Ministry, was the home of Judge William H. Battle while he taught law in Chapel Hill. It was sold to his son Kemp P. Battle and served as a president's house from 1876 to 1891. Battle established the South's first summer session for teachers (1877), an agricultural experiment station (1877), and a medical school (1879). After he relinquished the presidency he wrote a two-volume history of the University.

The name of the house is probably a pun on William Battle's name. Senlac was what the Normans called the spot where William the Conqueror fought the Battle of Hastings.

The president was exceptionally close to the students and cheered up those left behind at Christmas with entertainments and bonfires in the park.

It is related that Battle, while hiking in the mountains, approached a mountaineer to ask for lodging and identified himself as the president of the University. "That's all right," the man replied, "I'm just a plain man and mixing will learn us both." On another occasion, Battle chided a student who had attended an execution and ended, "Well, sir, consider yourself scolded and tell me all about the hanging."

Coker Arboretum

1903

The Coker Arboretum, a five-acre naturalistic garden containing four hundred varieties of ornamental plants and shrubs, was begun at the suggestion of President Francis P. Venable as he strolled along Senior Walk with botanist William C. Coker. The boggy area was then sown in crimson clover and grasses and for decades had been used as a pasture for campus beasts, most notably President Swain's white mule, Old Cuddy.

A pergola along Cameron Avenue is covered with wisteria, native yellow jessamine, and an ancient Banksia rose. Among the spectacular blooming trees are Marshall's thorn, river plum, red bud, red haw, and Japanese magnolia. Red fall-blooming spider lilies can be seen along Raleigh Street. Labeled for identification are a pistachio to the north of Senior Walk in the center of the garden and, across the path, a Walter's or cedar pine, which is rare for this area.

In recent years, there has been an emphasis on ornamental exotics such as dwarf evergreens. Beds of day lilies, camellias, and flowers of the Western United States have been added.

Coker was a leading authority on fungi; among his numerous studies was an internationally acclaimed work on the saprolegniaceae, the first publication to appear under the imprint of the UNC Press in 1923. As long-time head of the committee on buildings and grounds, Coker created a "monument in wisteria, iris, dogwood, and quince."

Davie Hall

1908, 1962

Davie Hall, now the Department of Psychology, was built as a belated tribute to the "Father of the University," William Richardson Davie, to house the Departments of Biology and Botany. The present structure, with its contemporary concrete facade, replaces a portion of the first building.

Davie was a legislator, a governor, and a treaty maker with Napoleon's government and with the American Indians, but he always thought of himself as a soldier of the Revolution, in which he served on four occasions.

He took unauthorized leave from Princeton University to join Washington's army at Elizabethtown, N.J. Shortly after graduation in 1776, he joined the North Carolina militia attached to the legion of Count Casimir Pulaski. Later, he equipped his own cavalry troop. At twenty-five he served his fourth hitch in the Revolution and was appointed acting commissary general to Nathanael Greene. It was his job to supply Greene's army without benefit of a single dollar in the military chest, as he had done for his own troop. Davie grumbled that he had become "a purveyor of beef and bacon, an inspector of invoices, a contractor for salt and tobacco." Andrew Jackson, then thirteen, was Davie's mounted orderly.

At thirty Davie was appointed to the Philadelphia Federal Convention of 1787 which wrote the United States Constitution; his vote there on the question of equal representation in the Senate regardless of state size was called "one of the most decisive votes ever cast in any constituent body—it made possible the success of the convention and constitution."

When Davie was elected to the North Carolina House of Representatives, he initiated a chain of events that resulted in twenty-three years of service to the University of North Carolina, most important of which was sponsoring the bill chartering the University.

Davie put up with no nonsense at

the University. It is said that he delayed the growth of drama at Chapel Hill for more than a century when, in 1796, after the first dramatic performances given at any state university in North America, Davie wrote peremptorily, "If the faculty insist on this kind of exhibition, the trustees must interfere. Our object is to make the students men, not players."

Again, when rebellion broke out, he wrote about the "presumption and loose manners of our young men . . . [who] affect to judge for themselves the trustees and even their parents in matters of morality, of government, of too much legislation, education, in fact everything. Nothing can be more ridiculous than boys at school talking of sacred regard for their rights. . . ."

In 1799 and 1800, Davie was furnished with $5,000 in gold and was sent to France by President John Adams as one of three ministers plenipotentiary to negotiate a treaty to end an undeclared naval war France had been waging on the new nation. The French negotiating team was headed by Citizen Joseph Bonaparte, and several times during the course of the year Davie was received by Napoleon who is said to have taken "uncommon notice of Davie . . . and thought him a great man."

Davie knew many of the eminent men of his day. He dined at Mount Vernon only three months before General Washington's death, and he met frequently with President John Adams. Eli Whitney once called at the Davie plantation to sell a cotton gin. Davie's hatred of England remained until the end, and he reflected the custom of some patriots who named their sons for cruel oriental despots, simply because they, too, had fought the old enemy. Davie's oldest son was named Hyder Ali, and two other prominent citizens sired Tippoo Saib Henderson and Tippoo Saib Haughton.

WALK 2

Starting at the north
end of McCorkle Place;
ending at the Ackland
Art Museum

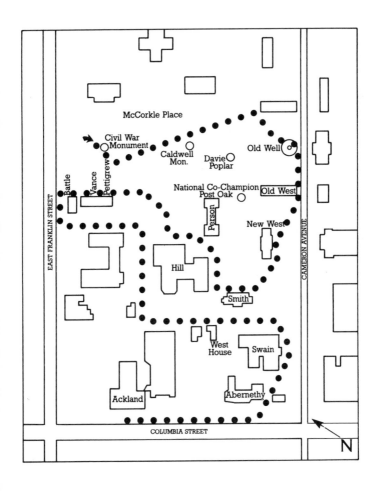

McCorkle Place

The stately wooded mall between Cameron and Franklin, the oldest portion of the campus, is known as McCorkle Place to honor the Reverend Samuel E. McCorkle, eighteenth-century teacher and Presbyterian clergyman who played many roles in the creation of the University. Four of the University's most revered landmarks define the axis of the campus there: the Old Well, the Davie Poplar, the Caldwell Monument, and the Civil War Monument.

Although McCorkle was not a member of the touring site-selection committee, he was involved in pinpointing the most desirable area of the state and ratifying the final choice. He influenced the planning of the University in the quadrangle tradition of Great Britain rather than in the trustee-favored fashion of Orientalization in which all buildings faced east, a style that may have had its origin in the Masonic order.

One of the few founding trustees with a college education, McCorkle *was depended on for decisions in academic planning. He shaped the first curriculum and wrote the first draft of the University's bylaws. Being the moralist among the trustees, he specified that the University be located remote from centers of population and thus "inaccessible to vice."*

Dr. McCorkle gave the oration at the cornerstone laying for Old East, at which time he said, "May this hill be for religion as the ancient hill of Zion, and for literature and the muses may it surpass the ancient Parnassus. . . . We hope ere long to see stately walls and spires ascending to [its] summit . . . adorned with an elegant village, accommodated with all the necessaries and conveniences of civilized society."

The symbol of the twin hills of Zion and Parnassus was a favorite of Dr. McCorkle's, for he used these names in hyphenated form for his excellent preparatory school near Salisbury, N.C. Here he combined classical and religious training and instituted a teacher-training pro-

gram that came to be regarded as the first normal school in America. Six of the seven graduates in UNC's first class of 1798 had done their preparatory work at Zion-Parnassus; only Hinton James, the very first student, was not a McCorkle product.

Dr. McCorkle also raised money for UNC. One of the institution's earliest gifts was $42.00 from McCorkle's church, "the only instance of congregational help in those early days."

Dr. McCorkle was considered the top contender for the job of first presiding professor of the University, but he was not chosen because of opposition from William R. Davie, a freethinker who distrusted preachers generally and Dr. McCorkle's executive ability in particular.

The minister was a close friend of General William Lee Davidson, for whom Davidson College was named. The general was wearing McCorkle's overcoat when he was killed fighting against Cornwallis on 1 February 1781. Hurley's Prophet of Zion-Parnassus reports that McCorkle's mother-in-law, an ardent colonial patriot, "relieved General Nathanael Greene in his hour of need by the gift of bags of gold." She had a private grudge against the British, however, for she bequeathed to McCorkle "my Negro fellow Dick that went off with the British in case he can ever be recovered."

McCorkle is said to have resembled Thomas Jefferson to a marked degree, and during a visit to Philadelphia the two were introduced. Both are said to have "retired from the interview with expressions of satisfaction."

McCorkle attended Princeton during the time that Aaron Burr's father was president.

Civil War Monument

This marker, erected in 1913 by the North Carolina Division of the United Daughters of the Confederacy, memorializes the 321 alumni of the University who died in the Civil War, as well as the 1,062 who entered the Confederate Army. On the north face of the monument, a heroic woman with sword in hand touches the shoulder of a young gentleman to call him from letters to arms. According to Robert Bingham, the Confederate soldier atop the marker is in full battle uniform, "but with no cartridge box."

The war touched the University immediately. Students rushed home to enlist as each of their states seceded. President Swain was determined, however, to hold the University together and managed to do so with boys under eighteen, wounded veterans, and those who were exempt. In 1863, when UNC enrollment was down to sixty-three, President Jefferson Davis eased the conscription law for students, saying he "would not grind up the seed corn." The UNC commencement of 1865, only two months after the cessation of hostilities, is thought to be the only graduation held at a Southern institution of rank in that year, and only four of the fifteen graduates were present. Thirty-five Federal soldiers stood guard at the exercises.

Chapel Hill was spared the devastation of battle. Although rifle pits were dug below Point Prospect, they were never used.

Caldwell Monument

Lying at the eastern base of this white marble obelisk are the University's first president, Joseph Caldwell; his second wife, Helen Hogg Hooper, daughter of one of the commissioners who selected the site of the University; and a son by her first marriage, Dr. William Hooper, grandson and namesake of the signer of the Declaration of Independence, who was a faculty member in ancient languages at varying periods between 1810 and 1837. For many years, commencement processions acknowledged the marker as they passed.

The symbols on the stone represent Dr. Caldwell's services to the state and to religion. A railroad wheel commemorates his advocacy of rail transportation in North Carolina, an engineer's transit records his work in locating the southern boundary of the state, and the Holy Bible suggests his many years as an ordained Presbyterian minister.

Caldwell was originally buried in the village cemetery, but over the following seventy-year period the body was exhumed three times, first for preparation of a death mask and twice for relocation on the campus. The marble obelisk replaces the original sandstone shaft that began to crumble and was removed to the village cemetery where it marks the graves of three faithful servants of the University— November and Wilson Caldwell, father and son, both slaves of the president, and David Barham.

Davie Poplar

This venerable ivy-clad tree predates the University, and the legends that have grown up around it are evidence of the rich inventiveness of the Southern oral tradition. Most of the stories suggest that Davie personally located the University lands around the tree, but the facts do not bear this out. The name Davie was assigned to the tree almost a century later by Cornelia Phillips Spencer, to commemorate one of the apocryphal tales.

Next to the tree, which is actually a tulip poplar, stands the Davie Poplar, Jr., a shoot grafted from the parent and planted by the class of 1918 when it was feared that the older tree would not survive having been struck by lightning.

The Davie Poplar has been one of the rallying places of the University for at least 190 years. The most noteworthy gathering beneath its branches took place at the commencement of 1859 when President James Buchanan and his Secretary of the Interior Jacob Thompson, a UNC graduate of 1831, stood in a reception line "shaded by this historic tree, then in its vigor and beauty, before the lightning and fierce wind had shattered it."

The late Tom Collins, syndicated columnist, wrote this about the poplar: "[It] is now chock full of cement, which with some cables is all that's holding it up. But it shall not fall before America does."

Here are some of the legends about the poplar:

It is said that in 1791 Davie tied his horse to the tree while he went to a spring to get water to weaken his brandy; hence, Davie Poplar.

Some have believed that Davie and the site-selection committee met at the spring in 1792 and had a picnic lunch accompanied by exhilarating beverages. Afterwards Davie pronounced, "This is it," and thrust a poplar branch into the ground to mark the place. The switch grew into the Davie Poplar. (Unfortunately for this tale, Davie was not on the committee.)

Most campus storytellers agree, however, that the tree was fully grown at the time of the trustees' visit—without Davie.

There were sound geographic reasons for the choice of Chapel Hill as the seat of the University. It stood on an eminence of granite belonging to the Laurentian system, where the main roads of the state crossed. At the crossroads stood a chapel of the Church of England, which gave the region its name, New Hope Chapel Hill. The legislature had specified that the University should not be within five miles of the seat of government or any court of law, probably because of the rowdiness that accompanied court week. Chapel Hill was a proper distance from both Raleigh and Hillsborough.

President Kemp Battle described the trustees' horseback journeys in search of a site in November 1792 as follows: "when the forests were clothed in their changing hues of russet and green, gold and crimson . . . and the hospitable farmers welcomed them with hearty greetings, and the good ladies brought out their foamiest cider and sweetest courtesies, while on the sideboard, according to the bad customs of that day, stood decanters of dark hued rum and ruddy apple brandy and the fiery juice of the Indian corn, which delights to flow in the shining of the moon."

Old Well

At the heart of the campus stands the visual symbol of the University of North Carolina, pictured frequently on University literature, Christmas cards, and student souvenirs. For many years the Old Well served as the sole water supply for Old East and Old West dormitories, which gave rise to the campus joke that the only place in Chapel Hill you could get a bath was in the jail. The well was given its present decorative form in 1897 at the suggestion of President Edwin A. Alderman, who was later president of Tulane and the University of Virginia. In 1954 the well was given added beauty with brick walks, plantings, and benches.

President Alderman described his beautification project: "I had always admired the little round temples which one sees reproduced so often in English gardens . . . derived largely from the Temple of Love in the Garden of Versailles. This Temple of Love was lineally descended—1. From a Greek shrine, 2. From the Tholos at Epidaurus, 3. From the Temple of Vesta at Tivoli, 4. From the 'Pietro Montorio' by Bramanti. Our little well is, therefore, a sort of sixth cousin of a Greek shrine, or third cousin of the Temple of Vesta, or second cousin of the Temple of Versailles." A local lumberyard constructed it for $200.

Old West

1822, addition 1848, interior rebuilt 1923

Old West dormitory was planned as an architectural twin of Old East, but architect William Percival made certain improvements on both; a score of years later Alexander Jackson Davis of New York further modified their appearance.

It is said that Harvard's early buildings "looked as though they meant business, nothing more," and the comment applies equally to the University of North Carolina. The barren box shapes of the first buildings created an architectural morale for the campus which was quite in keeping with the plain living and high thinking that went on within.

Students were prohibited "from betting on horse races, nor [could they] keep cocks or fowl of any kind . . . raffle, play cards or dice, *keep a dog or firearms, have spirituous liquor in rooms without permission of president or faculty." No student could build a hut or retain one already built without permission, nor were they allowed to fish, hunt, or walk abroad on Sunday. Students were expelled for dueling; a boy could be expelled for associating with an expelled student.*

A magnificent tree stands in the V formed by paths running from Old West to Hill Hall and Old West to Person Hall. It has been registered with the American Forestry Association as a National Co-Champion Post Oak (Quercus stellata). The oak stands ninety-four feet high, spreads its crown about ninety-two feet, and measures more than one hundred fifty-three inches in diameter at the height of a person's chest.

New West

1859, remodeled 1926

Strongly resembling New East on the other side of the quadrangle, New West served a similar function of dormitory and literary society hall. The Dialectic Society was located on the third floor; the same room now is headquarters for the merged literary societies, the Di-Phi Senate. The rest of the building is used by the Department of Computer Science.

The Literary Societies, which exposed students to forensic and parliamentary problems, were organized in 1795 through the influence of tutor Charles V. Harris, a graduate of Princeton and a member of the renowned Whig Society there. The societies were the oldest student organizations in the South and nationally second in age to the Princeton groups.

The libraries of the societies for many years were far more extensive than the University collection. Before the Civil War the University owned 3,600 books, and the total of both societies was twice that number. The society rooms were once the showplaces of the campus, with unusual furnishings and portraits of members who became distinguished in public life. Among the painters represented in these rooms were W. Garl Browne, W. G. Randall, Sully, Eastman Johnson, the Peales, Steene, Strudwick, and Fields.

Mary Ann Smith Building

1901

Mary Ann Smith Building was designed as a dormitory for sixty-five students, erected with funds that became available in 1891, many years after the donor drew up her will. In 1861 Miss Smith provided that after her death the University should establish a professorial chair in industrial chemistry as well as scholarships for students. Smith Building is now used by the Operations Research and Systems Analysis group, Statistics, and Computer Science.

Miss Smith's will indicated an interest considerably in advance of her time, for there had been little prior experimental work in science. The document is additionally remarkable because it was written by a woman who later spent many years in an insane asylum.

President Kemp Battle wrote: "Miss Smith was, when her mind was sound, a woman of excellent judgment and high principles, unostentatious and of broad charity." She was the only child of Richard Smith, a merchant of Raleigh, who had accumulated a large estate by North Carolina standards of that day.

Miss Smith's ambitions for the application of chemical experimentation to industry were dramatically realized in the laboratory of Francis P. Venable, first holder of the Smith chair, when calcium carbide was identified there in 1893.

Person Hall

East wing 1797, central section 1886, west wing 1892, remodeled 1934, refurbished 1977

Person Hall, the second oldest state university building in the United States, has been a University in itself, for it has had at least fifteen different academic uses. At present, it is used by the Department of Music. Its first function was that of a chapel, and it also served as the town meeting place for the first forty years of Chapel Hill's life. This room in the east wing is now a small recital hall, containing a Schlicker tracker-action organ and several period keyboard instruments. One of the most notable architectural structures in Chapel Hill, its handmade brickwork in the style of Flemish bond should be noticed. Art objects displayed along its exterior are: (on the north) Anna Hyatt Huntington's bronze sculpture titled "Youth," in which a young man is subduing a horse; and (on the south) a statue of Stephen Langton, an English cardinal and archbishop of Canterbury who died in 1288, and two gargoyles that came from London's Big Ben as a gift to the

University in 1933 from Katherine Pendleton Arrington.

When Person Hall was remodeled and rededicated to art, its third-to-last incarnation, President Frank Porter Graham said, "This building, which helped to cradle the revolutionary idea of the University of the people . . . has been the nurturing home of a long line of schools and departments on their way to new and larger buildings. . . . Faith and failure, aspiration and frustration, but always dreams and struggle, have been in this little pile since the first bricks of the red clay of Orange County were laid for Person Hall in the last decade of the eighteenth century. Today it stands . . . with most of the original bricks and all of the original simple lines, the work of many hands, the blending of three centuries." In the early part of the nineteenth century, when the trustees were thinking of tearing it down, Professor Elisha Mitchell pled for the building, say-

ing, "It is not a splendid, but it is a very neat edifice."

In Person Hall was held what was probably the first Sunday School in North Carolina; in it, too, the boys of the University met for morning prayers at sunrise and evening prayers at five o'clock. Its platform gave equal hospitality to the sacred and the profane—to itinerant preachers, showmen, ventriloquists, Siamese twins, and artists in glass-chewing. It was the scene of the celebration of the National Jubilee on 4 July 1826, the semicentennial of the Declaration of Independence. From its platform North Carolina Justice William Gaston gave his famous address in condemnation of slavery thirty years before Fort Sumter.

UNC, the only state university to graduate students in the eighteenth century, held its first commencement in Person, "the first fruits of our National Institution," it was described. Even after graduation exercises were transferred to Gerrard Hall in 1837, all UNC diplomas awarded up to the time of the Civil War bore the original inscription—that they had been granted in "Aula Personica" in "Sacrarii-Mons," or Mount of the Chapel.

This was the chapel where students deposited the livestock—the calves, the goats, and professors' horses that had been sadly daubed with paint or sheared of their manes. The literary societies met there before they acquired their own meeting rooms, and even though the building was unheated in winter and the wind often poured through broken window panes, the clerks of each society were carefully instructed to "extinguish every candle, fasten the windows and lock the door upon adjournment." In 1933, the first Chapel Hill rehearsal of the North Carolina Symphony was held in Person Hall, with Percy Grainger as soloist. The building was once gutted by fire and on three occasions has had its shape and size changed by remodeling.

The works of art outside were installed during the time the building served as a gallery. The English statue and gargoyles were discovered by Mrs. Katherine Pendleton Arrington of Warrenton when she was visiting London in 1933 to be presented at the Court of St. James. She saw the carvings being removed from Big Ben and was told that, although they were only eighty years old, they had so deteriorated in the London weather that they were being replaced. By paying for the replacement stones, she was given the originals. Mrs. Arrington provided the major benefaction in the art gallery renovation to honor her brother, Milo M. Pendleton, class of 1902.

After the carvings were installed, a writer in the Tar Heel commented, "These unseeing stone eyes have watched a century of world history being made. They have seen Peel, Gladstone and Disraeli hurry past to plan the fate of the British Empire . . . they have seen the heart of Britain beat."

The sculpture of Anna Hyatt Huntington, whose "Youth" is seen on the north wall, also appears in two hundred museums in the United States, including the Metropolitan. The Chapel Hill bronze is a reduction from a larger limestone group done for the Brookgreen Gardens in South Carolina. The gardens were created by the Huntingtons to display an outline collection of nineteenth- and twentieth-century American sculpture.

General Thomas Person, a childless, wealthy planter of Granville County, gave $1,050 in "hard money," said to be paid in shining silver dollars, toward the finishing of the chapel. The trustees promised to erect a tablet in evidence of this gift, a text was drafted, and Person shrewdly gave an extra sum for the marker, but it never appeared. Mrs. Arrington provided the overdue tablet 130 years later. After Person Hall, no other building constructed by private funds appeared on the campus until the early 1900s when Carr and Mary

41

Ann Smith buildings were completed.

Person was a delegate to the first assembly of the people at New Bern in 1774 and a member of the Provincial Congress at Hillsborough in 1775 and again in 1776. He was among the patriots who drafted the Constitution of North Carolina, which included provision for the creation of a state University, was a member of the legislature that chartered the University, and became a member of its first Board of Trustees.

Hill Hall

1907, 1962

The unmistakable look of a Carnegie Library is present in the white sandstone and buff brick facade of Hill Hall, for that was its original function. Less than two decades after it was finished, however, it had outgrown its 200,000-volume capacity and a larger library was imperative. This structure was transformed in 1930 into Hill Music Hall, through the benevolence of John Sprunt Hill, class of 1889, who gave the four-manual Reuter organ and provided funds for remodeling the old bookstacks into an auditorium. A stipulation of the gift was that weekly concerts be held in the building, which gave rise to the widely known Tuesday Evening Concert Series. Among the musical premieres held in the hall have been a nationally televised first performance by the Carolina Choir of Dave Brubeck's jazz oratorio, *Light in the Wilderness*, with the composer in attendance.

The building contains historical instruments such as lutes, recorders, and viols; and an electronic studio with a Moog synthesizer. The music library ranks high among the nation's specialized collections and is the largest in the South. Hill Hall is the home of outstanding faculty performers and student groups that present a full spectrum of the literature from early music to jazz.

Battle-Vance-Pettigrew

1912

This three-part Tudor-style structure, originally a dormitory but now
general administrative offices, was
intended to resemble buildings at
the University of Pennsylvania. Offices include student financial aid
and the Johnston Scholarship Program. Notice the diamond-paned
oriel windows and the functional
gargoyle water spouts above them.
Each of the parts bears the name of
a Carolina hero of the Civil War or
Reconstruction periods.

*Kemp Plummer Battle, fifty-one
years a trustee at UNC, was president from 1876 to 1891 and author
of a two-volume history of the
institution.*

*Zebulon Baird Vance was twice
governor of North Carolina, a
United States senator, and a man of
wide public interest.*

*James Johnston Pettigrew, the
most romantic figure of the trio, was
first an outstanding undergraduate
and later a gifted, extremely young
Confederate general whose valor
at Gettysburg provides one of the
interesting footnotes to history.
Pickett's Charge at Cemetery
Ridge is generally conceded to be
the most northerly point reached
by Confederate troops. Pettigrew
partisans contend that the action
should more correctly be labeled
"Pettigrew's Charge," because, due
to an angle in the famed wall,
Pettigrew and his forces actually
established the high watermark of
the war. In this engagement
Pettigrew's regiment suffered the
heaviest loss on either side in a single battle of the war.*

West House

1935

This charming one-story, red brick colonial cottage, now used for computer science, was built by Kenneth S. Tanner, class of 1911, Rutherfordton, N.C., as a unique residential retreat for his son, two nephews, and other companions during their undergraduate years. In 1942 the house became the headquarters of the Carolina Volunteer Training Corps for the duration of World War II.

One of the secret, charming spots of the campus is the brick-walled garden, which is an oasis in the midst of parking lots. Candy-striped camellias are planted in the wall niches, and boxwood, acuba, and spring bulbs alternate with brick paving.

Evidence of the Tanner family interest in the University is the Tanner Award for excellent and inspirational teaching, which was established by Kenneth Tanner and others in 1952 in honor of his parents, Simpson Bobo Tanner and Lola Spencer Tanner. Preference is given to teachers of freshmen and sophomore students; the awards have been made annually since 1956.

Kenneth Tanner was one of the powers behind the growth of the textile industry in North Carolina. Tanner mills at Rutherfordton manufacture women's clothing of high quality.

Swain Hall

1913

Swain Hall, now headquarters for the Department of Radio, Television, and Motion Pictures as well as the studios of WUNC-TV and Radio, was first an eating commons, so it was inevitable that students then called it Swine Hall, an impartial comment on the quality of the food and the deportment of the diners. In 1935, Swain Hall saw its finest hour as a dining hall—in addition to serving 4,000 regular customers, it fed 1,500 Boy Scouts of North Carolina a total of 13,500 meals in a four-day period. In the year ending June 1938, Swain Hall served one million meals at an average cost of 25.3 cents.

The building is named for David Swain, who served as third president of the University from 1835 to 1868. Earlier he had been governor.

Swain's thirty-three years is the longest presidential tenure in the University's history. He stimulated the first law studies and steered many young men into public service. He greatly beautified the campus with plantings and stone walls, built two dormitories, and entertained three presidents of the United States at various commencements.

After keeping the University open during the Civil War, his role in peace was his undoing. He officially surrendered Raleigh to General Sherman, his daughter married the Union general whose troops occupied Chapel Hill, and Swain died—as a result of an accident with a high-spirited horse given him by General Sherman—under the cloud of collaboration with the Union forces and dismissal from the University by the Reconstruction government.

Abernethy Hall

1907

This hall, designed as a student infirmary, was named for Dr. Eric A. Abernethy, first official physician to the University. Today it houses activity in Extension and Continuing Education dedicated to the concept that the boundaries of the campus are the boundaries of the state. Extension work touches every trade and profession in North Carolina and indirectly reaches hundreds of thousands who never set foot on the campus.

Extension work was begun in 1907 under Louis Round Wilson, who sought to help high school teachers become librarians as well as better teachers. By 1911 the Extension Division acquired its first budget of $600 and was constituted in its present form in 1912. Over the *years it has engaged in such varied enterprises as the historical dramas "The Lost Colony" and "Unto These Hills," the North Carolina Symphony, the Great Decisions discussion series, theatre trips to London, a wide range of course work, civil defense, school services, audio-visual education, developmental disabilities training, education of prison inmates, and the like. The high school debating program has attracted national attention and has involved 34,000 participants in its first fifty years. The Extension Division has started teaching enterprises throughout the state which have grown into community colleges and has provided impetus for the founding of branches of the University at Charlotte and Wilmington.*

Ackland Art Museum

1958

This red brick building of modified Williamsburg design is surrounded by plantings in the Williamsburg style. Inside and to the left of the entrance is a marble sarcophagus containing the remains of the donor and inscribed, "He wanted the people of his native South to know and love the fine arts, 1855–1940." The recumbent figure is a bronze executed by Milton Hebald in 1961 in Rome.

The Ackland houses an internationally respected collection of more than 7,000 works representing the history of Western art from ancient Egypt to the present. Included are paintings by Delacroix, Rubens, Courbet, and Corot; sculpture by Arp, Degas, and Rodin; master drawings, prints, twentieth-century photography, and North Carolina folk art. Loan shows come from major museums throughout the country, and a wide variety of special activities relate to each of the exhibitions.

Valentin de Boulogne's *St. John the Evangelist* of the School of Caravaggio and Eugene Delacroix's *Cleopatra and the Servant* are often borrowed from the Ackland for shows elsewhere. The latter went to the Louvre for an exhibition marking the centennial of the artist's death. A sculpture, *The Young Raphael*, by Carriere Belleuse has also been loaned to the Louvre.

Several collections built by individual donors have come to the Ackland, including two Joseph Palmer Knapp rooms of period furniture with 400-year-old paneling, the W. E. Shipp collection of silver and decorative arts, the Dr. W. P. Jacocks collection of 1,200 prints, and the Burton Emmett collection totalling 5,000 prints, drawings, and sculptures.

The Ackland bequest is the most unusual in UNC's history, for it came from a man who was unknown to the University at the time of his death. A Raleigh News and Observer columnist wrote, "The Ackland will case is a strange one, as obviously was Ackland himself. You don't have to go back to the time he got mad with his brother and therefore changed his name to discover that."

Ackland, a Washington, D.C., lawyer and recluse, had made a will stating that his $1.5 million estate should establish an art center somewhere in the South. He named Duke, UNC, and Rollins as his choices and stipulated that the building house his mausoleum. Conversations with the Duke president encouraged him to make a second will, naming only Duke. The president died; Ackland died. The succeeding administration at Duke was unwilling to honor the mausoleum stipulation. The case was in court for nine years, with UNC,

Rollins, and nieces and nephews involved. O. Max Gardner, former governor, served the University without compensation in the case, and it was decided in favor of UNC.

Ackland's fortune was based on an even stranger line of inheritance. The money began with his mother's first husband, Isaac Franklin, who had acquired it on the slave-auction block. The $110,000 nucleus was legally owned by his half sister Emma Franklin, who died at ten, passing it on to Ackland, then a baby of two months.

Ackland's family home, Belmont, whose lawns were laid out after the style of Hampton Court, was later occupied by the Ward-Belmont School in Nashville, Tenn.

To the south of the Ackland is the Frank Borden and Barbara Lasater Hanes Art Center, a $6.1 million classroom and studio building. The contemporary structure with traditional touches was occupied in 1983 and dedicated to the Haneses in 1985. Frank Borden Hanes, class of

1942, a prize-winning author, journalist, and businessman, is the son of Robert M. Hanes (see Hanes Hall). Both Haneses honored in this building have been especially interested in the arts and in the library.

To the east of the building is a small Alumni Garden, the gift of Larry Goodrich, '47.

WALK 3

Starting at South
Building; ending at
Wilson Library

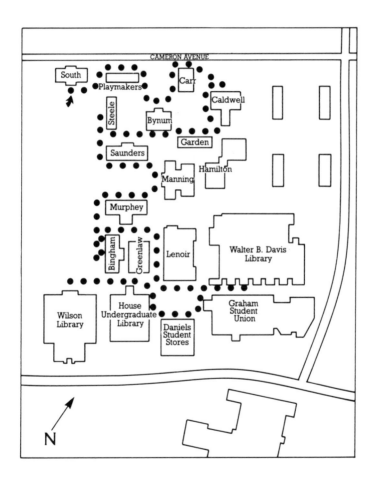

South Building

1798–1814, portico 1927

South Building stood roofless for sixteen years after its cornerstone was laid until financing could be completed by President Caldwell—who toured the state by stick-backed gig—and through a statewide lottery. It was originally a combined classroom and dormitory; its most eminent resident was President James Polk. It is now the central administration building.

The original plan called for South Building to be one wing of a much larger structure, but critics claimed this would be too vast for the University then projected. The grandiose scale of the plan prompted it to be labeled "the 'Temple of Folly' planned by the Demi-God Davie."

Although modeled after Nassau Hall at Princeton, South Building was austere at the outset. It has been softened over the years by a cupola added in 1861; a main doorway detail (1897) that was copied from Westover, the stately seventeenth-century home of William Byrd on the James River; and an Ionic portico (1926–27), designed by McKim, Mead, and White, to face Polk Place.

A wide variety of activity has taken place in South Building over the years. During the long period in which it stood unfinished, students built study huts inside its shell; these provided "quiet retreats in fair weather, but the skill of the occupants was not sufficient to protect them from rain."

On the second floor President Caldwell, between 1827 and 1831, conducted "the first systematic observations of the heavens known in the United States," while beneath the building Tom Jones, the campus licensed woodcutter, kept his axe and kindling. When Jones died suddenly without having time to arrange his earthly affairs, a substantial quantity of corn whiskey, a product he had been selling under the name "lightwood," was found beneath his woodpile. Horses and cows were stabled in South Build-

ing during the five years the University was closed during Reconstruction.

South Building's most distinguished tenant, James K. Polk, roomed with William D. Moseley, later governor of Florida, on the southwest corner of the third floor, where they were in the first class of students at the University to study conic sections. Moseley recalled that he and Polk also "spent many pleasant hours in reading together the Latin and Greek authors." Polk frequently elected to hike two miles to eat at a farmhouse on Bolin Creek rather than patronize the Steward's Hall on the campus.

Polk had a campus reputation for dependability. A student, impassioned in debate, once claimed that "his argument was just as true as the fact that Polk would arise in the morning at the first call."

Polk prepared for public life in the Dialectic Society, which he twice served as president. His inaugural address was on the topic

"Eloquence." Even his friends conceded that he had none.

The minutes of the society reveal that "Hamilton C. Jones was fined 10¢ for threatening language to James K. Polk and Polk the same for replying to Jones." Polk's portrait, painted by Thomas Sully during sittings done in the White House, now hangs in the Di-Phi Senate room.

In his first debate in the Dialectic Society in 1816, Polk attacked the idea of U.S. assistance to Spanish America in gaining liberty from Spain. Exactly ten years later, in his first session of Congress, Polk maintained the same position.

The president returned to his alma mater after twenty-nine years for the commencement of 1847, accompanied by his secretary of the navy, John Y. Mason, a UNC alumnus, and other dignitaries.

Miss Nancy Hilliard erected a special addition to her hotel to accommodate the presidential party, and students and faculty lined the

entrance walk there to welcome the celebrities as they arrived in carriages from Raleigh.

"President Polk was applauded for his total abstinence of ostentation," a contemporary wrote, "and his sincere and unassuming courtesy. The contrast with one of his classmates, who looked twenty years younger than Polk, was observed, [as was] the president's anxious countenance, his silvered hair and careworn features."

It is possible that the return to Chapel Hill was the social highlight of the Polks' four years in the White House. The Polks were not popular, and the White House was socially tranquil during his administration. "You would be surprised to see how little attention the President or his family receives here," a report from Washington noted. "If it were not for the office seekers, he would receive hardly any." No one saw them off when they left for Chapel Hill, so the welcome on the campus must have been doubly gratifying.

The conduct of a lottery for public causes, such as for the completion of South Building, was not uncommon; "the public conscience of the day saw no harm in calling in the aid of the Goddess Fortuna for promoting religion, education or any other desirable end." Tickets were sold for $5.00 and General Lawrence Baker, grandfather of the Confederate general of the same name, won $1,500, while the University profited by $5,080.81.

A contractor with the appropriate name of John Close, "who was near in his calculations," completed the building at the time the nation was going crazy with jubilation over naval victories against England. Students moved into the completed building to the roar of the first and last cannon fired in Chapel Hill.

Playmakers Theatre

1851, remodeled 1924, restored 1981

The most beautiful building on the Carolina campus, to many tastes, is this Greek Revival temple considered to be one of the masterworks of New York architect Alexander Jackson Davis. He designed the building as an unlikely combination library and ballroom; later it was used for agricultural chemistry and law. In 1925, this became the first state university building dedicated to the making of native dramatic art through the American folk play. The regional theater work of the Carolina Playmakers on the campus dates from 1918.

Instead of the acanthus leaves that usually ornament Corinthian capitals, Davis substituted wheat and Indian corn, in response to the aggressive Americanism then present in the country. Bricks for the building were provided by the Episcopal rector, who ran that business on the side.

The building was named for Benjamin Smith, the University's first major donor. It was designated a National Historic Landmark in 1974.

A persistent but unsubstantiated campus legend has it that the horses of the Michigan Ninth Cavalry were stabled in the library after the Civil War. This stimulated the story that, since then, Michigan horses have been known for their intelligence and Carolina students for their horse sense.

The Carolina Playmakers, founded by Professor Frederick Koch, have launched alumni and associates into many branches of the arts. They include Thomas Wolfe, whose first love was playwrighting and who performed the title role in his student-written play The Return of Buck Gavin; *Pulitzer Prize-winning playwright Paul Green; comedian Andy Griffith; band leader Kay Kyser; actor Sheppard Strudwick, Academy Award-winning actress Louise Fletcher; and authors Richard Adler (*Pajama Game *and* Damn Yankees*),* Betty Smith (A Tree Grows in Brooklyn*), and Frances Gray Patton (*Good Morning, Miss Dove*). Today's PlayMakers Repertory Com-*

pany is a not-for-profit Equity Theatre.

Benjamin Smith, special aide to General Washington during the Revolution and state senator and governor of North Carolina, gave 20,000 acres of land warrants in northwestern Tennesse to the University at the first meeting of the Board of Trustees.

Many years of litigation passed before the lands were ready to be sold, and during this time an earthquake called "Old Shaker" covered 15,000 of Smith's acres with water. The remaining land was sold for $4,000, a sadly diminished first major benefaction to the University.

As Smith grew older, he became irascible and prone to resent fancied slights. As a result he became involved in a duel with a younger man and received a bullet in the side which he carried until his death. He was sent to debtors' prison, where he remained until the University trustees ordered his release. Even after death, his body was pursued by hungry creditors, a barbaric custom then allowed by law. His friends buried him at night in an obscure spot, where the money ghouls could not find him.

Bynum Hall

1904

The campus's first professionally equipped gymnasium was given by Judge William Preston Bynum (1820–1909) as a memorial to his grandson and namesake, William Preston Bynum, Jr., a Carolina football player in the class of 1893 who died of typhoid fever at the end of his sophomore year.

Before the construction of Bynum Hall, an indoor gymnasium had been improvised in the first Memorial Hall, but it had no dressing rooms, heat, or baths. Bynum Hall changed all this; its indoor pool was the pride of the campus—until it was declared unsanitary for lack of a filter system.

Today Bynum houses administrative functions such as the Graduate School, Affirmative Action Office, the News Bureau, and University Cashier.

When Bynum Hall was presented to the University, a trustee stated, "There could not have been devised a more fitting memorial to a college boy than this. Not infrequently one hears some one say that boys are sent to college to study, not to play ball. Such are incapable of feeling the wild delight that follows upon a home run in the ninth with a short score and the bases full, or the delirious joy of the touchdown which brings victory. . . . Boys should go to college to study and to play ball, if they are to reap the full benefits of the course."

Carr Building

1899

Carr Building, designed in the Richardson Romanesque style with heavy entrance arches, was constructed as a dormitory, largely with funds given by Julian Shakespeare Carr of Durham. It was the largest building gift received by the University up to that time. The University Housing Office is located here. Notice the red ceramic gargoyles on the south and west gables.

Carr was one of North Carolina's first big-league businessmen; he was the aggressive advertiser who plastered the picture of Bull Durham tobacco all over the world.

It may be, however, that his largest international impact came with the education of a homeless Chinese boy named Soong Chiao-chun (Charlie Soong), perhaps the most famous foreign student ever to study in North Carolina.

Fourteen-year-old Soong ran away from a Boston uncle who had decided to make him into a silk and tea merchant. He was first be- *friended by a sea captain who brought him to Wilmington, N.C., then by a Methodist minister who baptized him in the Christian faith, and finally by Carr who took him into his Durham home and educated him at Trinity College and Vanderbilt Theological School. Soong later became an official in the Kuomintang, was treasurer of the Chinese Revolution of 1911, and founded a powerful twentieth-century dynasty. His three daughters became the wives of Generalissimo Chiang Kai-shek, Dr. Sun Yat-sen, and H. H. Kung, and his three sons were eminent in banking.*

When Carr visited Shanghai, Charlie Soong, who had once woven hammocks in his room at the Carr home to help pay his way in America, brought the leaders of new China to pay their respects. Sun Yat-sen presented Carr with three specially designed vases as a gift of the Chinese government.

When the twenty-five-old Carr entered the tobacco business in 1870, he inaugurated an advertising

campaign that put the Durham Bull on the walls and rooftops of the world, leading Mark Twain to observe dryly that the most conspicuous thing about the Egyptian pyramids was the Bull. It is alleged that the baseball term "bull pen" was coined because the Bull was painted behind the dugout of the New York Yankees. Carr arranged newspaper advertising showing Alfred Lord Tennyson smoking Bull Durham with Prime Minister Gladstone; other Bull enthusiasts were James Russell Lowell and Thomas Carlyle, who "wrote the mad humors and violent tropes of the French Revolution while enjoying the pungent bite of the Bull."

The Bull was highly conspicuous at home as well. The factory whistle sounded like the greatly amplified roar of a bull and each time it roared the cost to the company was $8.00.

Carr befriended a wide range of individuals and institutions. He made it possible for Josephus Daniels to buy the Raleigh News and Observer, and he loaned money to John Merrick, pioneer Negro capitalist, to start him in a business career. Carr's hosiery plant was the first textile plant in the nation to employ Negroes. He was the first man from the South to make a donation to any northern educational institution after the war when he gave $10,000 to American University in Washington.

His largest benefactions were in North Carolina, however, where he is credited with saving Trinity College, now Duke University, and Greensboro Female College. He gave sixty acres of land for the Durham site for Trinity College, bringing it in from the country, and Washington Duke put up the money.

Twice he loaded the entire North Carolina Masonic Lodge onto horse-drawn wagons and hauled them from Durham to Chapel Hill for the UNC commencement. The Masons puffed long clay pipes filled with Bull Durham as they made their ceremonial entrance along Franklin Street.

Caldwell Hall

1911

Caldwell Hall has successively housed medicine, pharmacy, and public health. It was named for Joseph Caldwell, first president of the University—although he was involved in none of the medical disciplines—some seventy-five years after the decision had been reached to honor him in this manner. The building has some elements of the Renaissance style. Today the building houses the Department of Philosophy, and some special programs, such as Women's and International Studies.

Caldwell was an ordained Presbyterian minister, but his consuming interests were mathematics, engineering, and astronomy. He had graduated at nineteen with highest honors from Princeton and at UNC became one of the pioneers in astronomical science in America. The observatory he built in 1831 near the village graveyard was the second on a campus, preceded only by one at the College of William and Mary. Shortly after Caldwell's death, the observatory was destroyed by student arson. It was not rebuilt, but the sound bricks remaining were reused to build a kitchen for President Swain.

Before Caldwell acquired his observatory, however, he made his first astronomical observations on the second floor of South Building, determining that its position was 35°54'2"N and 79°17'W. Atop the president's house he built a platform and took seniors up to view the heavens in groups of three or four.

He placed a sundial in the presidential garden which stood until Sherman's bummers arrived in 1865, and he erected meridian pillars in the yard which still stand covered by vines, showing on their eastern and western faces the true north-south line of his day.

Hamilton Hall

1972

Contemporary high-rise Hamilton Hall houses history, sociology, political science, the Institute for Latin American Studies, and a number of special curriculums. The building is named for Joseph Gregoire deRoulhac Hamilton, a faculty member from 1906 to 1948 and a Kenan professor, who founded the Southern Historical Collection.

The Southern Historical Collection (located in Wilson Library) was officially established by the Board of Trustees in 1930, although Hamilton had begun collecting on a part-time basis in 1927. A modest collection of papers had also been made in the nineteenth century under presidents David Swain and Kemp Plummer Battle.

Hamilton traveled hundreds of thousands of miles all over the South, searching barns and garrets for manuscripts in his endless pursuit of history. He was appalled when he discovered that a ton and a half of papers had been destroyed in Fayetteville from a family active in public life and the newspaper world; he was horrified when he learned that two thousand letters of Benjamin Hedrick, controversial UNC professor, had been burned. The granddaughter of General Zachary Taylor told Hamilton in 1936 that she would "hunt up the rest of the letters, steal them . . . if necessary, and lie about it afterwards!" The work of "Ransack" Hamilton did not go unnoticed by collectors in other states. One Southern historian observed, "When Dr. Hamilton came along and gathered up enough of their papers to make them infernally mad, they got busy and are now doing something on their home grounds."

A small fenced garden has been developed near Hamilton Hall, designed to be enjoyed from the high-rise building.

Steele Building

1920

Steele Building, now housing administrative offices for student affairs, the first to face the newly planned Polk Place, was a dormitory until 1957 when it was remodeled for University offices, among them the deans of men and women and part of the graduate school. Notice the rising sun above the doorways, "expressive of education in the state, and emblem of Apollo, the God of Eloquence." The building was named for Walter Leak Steele, secretary of the Secession Convention of 1861, and a trustee active in reopening the University.

Steele exemplified an anecdote told of Professor Elisha Mitchell, one of UNC's great teachers, who had a notably soft heart toward errant boys. In matters of discipline he would often urge, "Let him go! Let him go! He is good legislature and trustee material."

Mitchell reclaimed Steele for education after a six-month suspension, and only two years after graduation he was elected to the General Assembly. In 1852, at the ripe age of twenty-nine, he became a state senator and a trustee of the institution from which he had been suspended a decade earlier.

Steele had a perfect memory for minute detail and was reputed to be the best chess player in North Carolina. Politics and law dominated much of his life; he became a congressman, president of a cotton mill, and president of the Alumni Association.

Saunders Hall

1922

In Saunders, now housing the departments of Religious Studies and Geography, and its twin, Murphey Hall, the University made its first attempt at air cooling for the summer months. It was no more successful than the plan for centrally heating New East and New West had been before the Civil War. A collection of domestic archaeological artifacts which range in age from the tenth to the third centuries before Christ, excavated in Israel by expeditions co-directed by the late Bernard Boyd, may be seen in room 101 and the nearby hall. Saunders is named for William Lawrence Saunders, cofounder of the *Raleigh News and Observer* and North Carolina's secretary of state, who spent eleven years compiling and editing *The Colonial Records of North Carolina*.

It is probable that he was a militant leader of the Ku Klux Klan during Reconstruction. When word went out that he was being sought by U.S. authorities as Emperor of the Invisible Empire, he left for a fishing trip "in order to mature his plans and arrange his private matters before he should be arrested." Friends raised money and urged him to slip away to England. But he chose to return, was arrested, and was taken to Washington where he was examined by the Ku Klux Klan committee of Congress. He was asked more than one hundred questions; to each he gave the polite, monotonous rejoinder, "I decline to answer."

Manning Hall

1923

The Latin words "lex" and "ius"—law and rights—that flank the name Manning suggest this building's original use. It now contains the School of Library Science and the Institute for Research in Social Science. The traditional stateliness of the building is achieved by Ionic pillars, an impressive flight of steps, and a cupola. The building is named for John Manning, who in 1881 took charge of the Department of Law succeeding Judge William H. Battle.

"For twenty-nine years this one thing he did: he practiced law," Associate Justice William J. Adams of the North Carolina Supreme Court wrote of Manning. "He had no distracting political ambition and refused time after time to be enticed by the tinsel of public office."

The Institute for Research in Social Science, established in 1924 by the eminent Southern sociologist Howard W. Odum, is the oldest such academic research center in the United States. Social Forces, founded in 1922, was the South's first journal on that subject. Katherine Jocher, who began as a research assistant in the institute in 1923, was the first woman in a major Southern university to work her way through the ranks to full professor.

Murphey Hall

1922

Murphey Hall, home of the Department of Classics, resembles Saunders, which is across the east arm of the quadrangle; the graceful fanlights above both their main entrances should be noticed. The building is named for Archibald DeBow Murphey, a nineteenth-century prophet whose visions later became public policy for the state.

Murphey died a failure, however. He had failed to establish a network of internal waterways for North Carolina's transportation system, he had failed to establish an idealistic plan for public education drawn heavily from ideas in Plato's Republic, and he had failed to complete his massive history of the state. He had also spent twenty days in debtors' prison, and because he had once been a judge, he was considered the most noted victim of an archaic, vindictive law.

When he was buried in Hillsborough, there was no money for a headstone, although he had once lived on a two-thousand-acre plantation manned by sixty slaves, and there had been a profitable mill and distillery on the place. In the plantation house was a library of two thousand books, and above the fireplace hung portraits of the master and mistress painted by Gilbert Stuart. In addition Murphey had once owned a sixteen-hundred-acre health resort with mineral springs and thousands of additional acres in North Carolina and Tennessee.

Murphey had "sought to awaken North Carolina to a knowledge of her own resources and character, to arouse a state pride that would bring to an end the westward emigration which was draining the population."

When North Carolina had become notorious for the highest illiteracy rate in the Union and enacted public education in 1840, it was to Murphey's model of 1817 that legislators turned.

Although the day of the railroad soon rendered obsolete the river-canal-turnpike system advocated

by Murphey, the topographical and statistical knowledge gained from the waterways study can be considered the first suggestion of a government-sponsored geological survey done in America.

In compiling the ten-volume Colonial Records of North Carolina, William L. Saunders worked with materials Murphey had persuaded the legislature to have copied in England in preparation for his own projected historical work.

Only belatedly did the name of Archibald DeBow Murphey become recognized. He was acknowledged as the "father of the public schools," and Murphey School buildings appeared in Raleigh, Greensboro, and Caswell County. In 1916 North Carolina Day in the public schools was designated as Murphey Day, and students were required to commit short passages of his writings to memory, to answer questions on Murphey's life and his significance to the state, and to contribute pennies and nickels for a marker for the town in Cherokee County which bears his name.

It is recorded that when Murphey was imprisoned for debt, he asked that his cell door be left open for light and ventilation. After it had remained open for several days, a caller pointed out that the law held the sheriff personally accountable for a prisoner's debt in such a case, since an open door technically constituted an escape even though the prisoner did not leave the premises. When this was brought to Murphey's attention, he said quietly, "Mr. Sheriff, my friend, it will be safest for you to lock the door upon me." As the sheriff complied, two tears rolled down his cheeks.

Bingham Hall

1929

Bingham Hall, home of the Department of Speech Communication and some work in English, was named for Robert Bingham, class of 1857, the fourth member of a distinguished North Carolina family to conduct a Bingham School at various locations in the state over a span of 130 years. Notice the two devices above the principal doorway, the seal of the University on the left and that of the state on the right. The institutional seal bears a shield, two torches of learning, and the motto "Lux Libertas." The shields are also seen on Saunders and Murphey halls.

Robert Bingham, for whom this building was named, dedicated his life to the cause of private preparatory education, but he was a great supporter of public schools as well. A number of his speeches gave early support to the founding of the present North Carolina State University at Raleigh and UNC at Greensboro.

The founder of the Bingham line of schoolmasters came to America from Ireland in the late eighteenth century when he heard that a headmaster's job was open in Wilmington, N.C. The ship delivered him to Wilmington, Del., however, and by the time Bingham got to North Carolina the job was filled. "In these straits," wrote Robert Bingham, "he gave the Masonic sign while drinking a glass of water, which was at once recognized and he was employed as a private tutor." The first Bingham School was founded in Pittsboro in 1795; the last closed in Asheville in 1929, not long after Robert Bingham's death.

Greenlaw Hall

1970

Five-story Greenlaw Hall is the headquarters for English, traditionally one of the largest of the University departments. It also includes offices for the curriculums in American Studies and in Folklore. The building is made of brick to harmonize with the traditional structures on either side but in general style relates to the contemporary buildings across the court. A contemporary feeling is achieved by vertical white concrete panels that dramatize the window shafts and by access areas overhung by the building itself. It memorializes Edwin A. Greenlaw, who held two of the most distinguished professorships in the United States. He was in the first group of Kenan Professors appointed at UNC in 1918, and he was the Sir William Osler Professor at The Johns Hopkins University at the time of his death.

Greenlaw was internationally known as a philologist and a scholar of medieval romance, Shakespeare, and Milton. His crowning achievement was the conception and planning of the Johns Hopkins Spenser variorum edition of the Faerie Queen. *A prodigious scholar whose published titles are numbered in the hundreds, he brought out a four-volume series called* Literature and Life *that was used in high schools throughout the nation.*

Under Greenlaw, the English department introduced journalism to the campus, stimulated creative work in drama, and gathered a distinguished group of scholars who gave it national distinction. When Greenlaw became dean of the graduate school, "he made the graduate school conscious of itself and the nation conscious of it."

Lenoir Hall

1939

Lenoir Hall was designed as an eating commons for 1,300 persons and started operation as a replacement for old Swain Hall in January 1940. It now contains University Dining Services and Aerospace Studies. The hall is named for General William Lenoir, Revolutionary patriot, who attended the first meeting of the University's Board of Trustees, was elected president at the second meeting, and was the last surviving member of the founders when he died fifty years after the enactment of the charter.

Lenoir was involved in General Rutherford's campaign against the Cherokees in 1776, and after hostilities began against Great Britain, he was constantly engaged in suppressing the Tories. He took part in the Battle of Kings Mountain, one of the significant engagements that advanced the American cause, and here had a brush with death when he was "shot through the hair above where it was tied."

Lenoir was a man of such great physical strength that at eighty-two he was still able to lift a wagon loaded with corn by putting his shoulder beneath it. At eighty-six he broke a bone in a fall from a horse; nevertheless, three weeks before his death at eighty-eight he rode fifty miles across the Blue Ridge Mountains to attend court. His name is also given to a county in eastern North Carolina, a town in the western part of the state, and a street in Raleigh.

Walter R. Davis Library

1983

The largest educational building in North Carolina, the Davis Library opened on 7 February 1984. Two students with a sense of history camped out in front of the library the night of 6 February so they could be the first users of the building. The $22.9-million structure, which includes several ingenious design features, has ten acres of floor space over nine levels on a three-acre site. One of the striking features is the spacious main gallery hung with colorful banners depicting historic printers' marks represented in the Rare Book Collection. Contemporary tapestries done by Durham artist Silvia Heyden which hang above the circulation desk are a gift of the class of 1983. The library was designed by the award-winning architects Leslie N. Boney of Wilmington and Romaldo Giurgola of Mitchell/Giurgola and Thorp of Philadelphia and New York. The latter designed a high-rise building in front of historic Independence Hall as well as the shelter for the Liberty Bell in Independence Square.

The building, which has a capacity of 1.8 million volumes, contains airy, light large spaces, as well as variation in ceiling height and in materials. A contemporary double arch appears in the unit housing the main reading room. There are 500 closed carrels, 144 faculty studies, and 1,950 open carrels and table seating. Total seating capacity is 3,013.

Walter R. Davis, for whom the building is named, is a Texas businessman with family roots in Elizabeth City, N.C. He was a member of the Board of Trustees for eight years and fought in the state legislature to claim for Chapel Hill the major portion of funds received from the sale of University utilities. A trustee resolution at the time the building was named read: "These good works are especially striking when one remembers that Walter Davis is not a graduate of this University."

Frank Porter Graham Student Union

1968, 1980

Financed entirely by student funds, this "home of creation and recreation" accommodates major student activities offices and student government. In the original building, on the lowest level, are twelve bowling lanes and a billiard room. Nearby is the office of the North Carolina Fellows program. On the main level is the Information Desk, the Great Hall, an art gallery, the International Student Center, and a snack bar. On the top level are student activities meeting rooms and the Frank Porter Graham Lounge. The new wing (1980) contains student publications, radio station WXYC, student legal services, and an auditorium that is the home of the Union's active film program. Outside, a brick terrace with umbrella-shaded tables overlooks an assembly area known as "The Pit." The building is named for Frank Porter Graham, eleventh president of the University.

Graham was a prime force in building the University in the 1930s. The Consolidated University of North Carolina was formed under his staunchly liberal administration, and he guided it through depression and war. Later he served as United States senator and as mediator for the United Nations, "a traveling salesman for world peace." The Saturday Evening Post *once described Graham as having one foot firmly planted on the Sermon on the Mount and the other on the Bill of Rights.*

Josephus Daniels Student Stores

1968

One of the most modern campus student stores in the United States, this contemporary structure is book-oriented. Texts are sold on the second floor, while on the first, in the Bulls Head Bookshop, there are thousands of titles for pleasure reading. Sharing the first floor is a large shop for school supplies and personal items. All income above operating expenses is contributed to scholarships and grants. The building memorializes Josephus Daniels, secretary of the navy in Woodrow Wilson's cabinet, publisher of the *Raleigh News and Observer*, and longtime University trustee.

During World War I, Daniels transferred two million doughboys to France. President Franklin Roosevelt, who had been Daniels's assistant during that period, always referred to him as "Chief" and appointed him ambassador to Mexico.

Daniels felt that one of his main responsibilities as a newspaper publisher was criticism of the government. The Greensboro Daily News *once reported that a frustrated Republican in the General Assembly threatened, "We are going to take the state capitol to Greensboro and leave nothing in Raleigh but the State Penitentiary, the State Insane Asylum, and Josephus Daniels." To this the editor replied, "These are the three institutions which are necessary to keep Republicans straight."*

The Observer *so accurately reflected the opinion and sentiment of a locality that it became a national institution.*

Robert B. House Undergraduate Library

1968

This building houses 125,000 books of particular significance for college-level work. More than 1,700 seats are available for study, 630 of them in private carrel spaces. In addition to general reading rooms, there are areas for typing, microfilm study, and the use of a nonprint collection made up of audiovisual materials. The library gives extensive instruction to undergraduates on the best use of the building's resources. The fully air-conditioned, carpeted, open-plan building has elevators for the handicapped and computerized book circulation. The building is named for Chancellor Emeritus Robert B. House.

Robert House served for over thirty years as an administrator. He was appointed the University's first chancellor in 1945 and in retirement taught in the English department.

His loyalty to Carolina was legend. He once said to a professor who was leaving for higher pay elsewhere: "You may go if you like. But I have enlisted for life. And if everybody else departs I expect to go up to Old South Building every morning, ring the college bell, knock the ashes out of my pipe, and lecture to the birds, the squirrels and the trees on the state of the universe and the University."

House, who wrote the book Aunt Sue and the Sheriff *based on his boyhood in Halifax County, commented, "I've been working at something ever since the age of eight, when I got my first job as nursemaid and butler to a jersey cow." He is locally famous as a harmonica player.*

Louis Round Wilson Library

1929, additions in 1952 and 1977

The Wilson Library, which served for fifty-five years as the research library in the humanities and social sciences, is now dedicated to special collections. It is named for Louis Round Wilson, a Kenan professor and a University librarian for thirty-one years, during which time he was the first director of the UNC Press, first editor of the *Alumni Review*, a planner of the School of Library Science and of the Extension Division. He died in 1979, several weeks short of his 103rd birthday. *Time* magazine called him "the peppery gadfly."

Foremost among the special resources of the building is the Southern Historical Collection of eight million manuscripts. It was the first manuscript repository dedicated to gathering materials from an entire region of the nation.

The Rare Book Collection contains special groups such as the Hanes Collection of Incunabula, including the ceremonial volumes that mark the millions in the library's holdings. The three millionth book was presented in fall 1983.

The North Carolina Collection dates to an effort begun in 1844, and today contains more than 170,000 books and pamphlets—the most comprehensive group of published materials on any one of the United States. Scheduled for completion in 1986 is a new reading room, as well as a Thomas Wolfe area, a North Caroliniana gallery and exhibition area, and a replica of the many-sided library in historic Hayes Plantation near Edenton, owned by Governor Samuel Johnston, first person to be named to the University board of trustees and its first chairman. Also of interest are the Sir Walter Raleigh Rooms and the Early Carolina Rooms.

WALK 4

Starting at the south
end of Polk Place;
ending at the Carolina
Inn

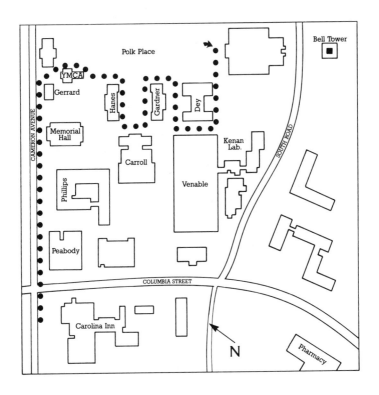

Polk Place

Polk Place, around which the south campus was developed, is named for UNC's most famous son, James K. Polk, eleventh president of the United States, whose room in South Building overlooked this area. During the building surge that took place between 1921 and 1931, the University made a fresh start southward with a cross-shaped quadrangle; its buildings were designed in reinterpreted colonial or modified Georgian fashion. The architectural firm of McKim, Mead, and White was consultant for the master plan. The colonial style was maintained as the University's official architecture until the 1960s.

Polk was the first dark horse in American political life, named as a candidate because the convention was deadlocked. He did not seek office, and even before he moved into the White House, he announced that he would not serve a second term. He was called "the dullard president," but the twentieth century has taken a new look at him, particularly after the publication of his diary in 1910. At mid-century Arthur Schlesinger, Sr., asked fifty-five historians to choose the ten greatest presidents, and Polk showed up as tenth on the list, immediately following John Quincy Adams. Polk's greatest service to the nation was rounding out the Pacific Coast line. Sam Houston once observed that the only thing wrong with the teetotaling Polk was that he drank too much water.

William Rand Kenan, Jr., Laboratories

1971

These chemistry laboratories, occupying a contemporary concrete ten-story triple-section tower that is partially joined to Venable Hall, were completed at a cost of $4.6 million and enabled the University to double its graduate enrollment in chemistry. The laboratories, totaling 130,000 square feet, mark chemistry's passing from the test tube to the vacuum tube and contain sophisticated electronic instruments that require vibration-free environments, air conditioning, and extensive wiring.

When William Rand Kenan, Jr., died in 1965, he left an estate of $100 million derived from railroads, hotels, and steam and electric generating plants. As a student laboratory assistant he was involved in identifying calcium carbide, one of the great discoveries of the age. He installed the first electric power plant in Chapel Hill and later introduced carbide lights throughout the world. Kenan was deeply interested in the athletic program at UNC and made several gifts totaling more than a million dollars to build and enlarge beautiful Kenan Stadium in memory of his parents. The stadium, seating 43,000, is located across South Road and a bit east of Kenan Laboratories. Through a charitable trust Kenan provided that $5 million be added to the Kenan Professorship program established earlier by other members of his family. He also gave an experimental farm to North Carolina State University at Raleigh.

Venable Hall

1925, 1953, 1983

Venable Hall is home to a department that in the past decade has generally trained more baccalaureate degree chemists than any other university in the nation. The first two red brick Venable structures, in themselves a 2.5-acre plant, have been augmented by a four-story undergraduate teaching laboratory building scheduled for completion in 1985. This laboratory's textured concrete exterior resembles Kenan Laboratories. Two former chairmen of the department, Dr. Francis P. Venable and Dr. Charles H. Herty, were presidents of the American Chemical Society.

Dr. Venable, president of the University from 1900 to 1914, was among the first five Kenan professors to be appointed at UNC. He was associated with two important industrial discoveries but derived no direct financial return from either. In 1886 he devised the present form of the Bunsen burner but sold his rights for six of the burners. In 1893 his laboratory was the scene of the identification of calcium carbide, the material from which acetylene is made. The substance had been produced in Spray, N.C., by recent graduate John Motley Morehead; working in the campus laboratory under Dr. Venable was William Rand Kenan, Jr. Both Morehead and Kenan later became captains of industry and major benefactors of the University.

William M. Dey Hall

1962

The original portion of this air-conditioned building, first opened for classes in the summer of 1962, is named for William Morton Dey, chairman for forty years of Romance languages and a Kenan professor. It contains the departments of Germanic, Romance, and Slavic Languages, as well as work in linguistics and in comparative literature.

"Dr. Billy" became famous shortly after his arrival in 1909 for "The French Revolution"—his dramatic raising of departmental standards so that it became one of the best in the nation. He faced a campus rebellion at the outset but succeeded in making "students out of enrollees."

Shortly after his retirement in 1949, Dey became the South's first Chevalier of the French Legion of Honor in recognition of services rendered in French culture and language as well as his own scholarly work and teaching. The medal was carried in Dr. Dey's funeral procession.

Under Dr. Dey the department's teaching staff grew from three to sixty, turned out large numbers of teachers, sent men to diplomatic service, and during World War II was virtually decimated to furnish interpreters, translators, intelligence, and censorship officials.

Dr. Dey was one of the founders of Studies in Philology, founded the Publications of the Department of Romance Languages, was faculty marshal for fourteen years, and from 1935 to 1940 served as first chairman of the Division of Humanities.

O. Max Gardner Hall

1953

Classwork in economics is centered in Gardner Hall. The building is named for a man who was concerned with economic problems throughout his lifetime as lawyer, textile executive, and depression governor of North Carolina. As governor he preserved the credit of North Carolina, established the state's responsibility for roads, and added $50 million to the agricultural wealth through his "live at home" campaign.

Later in life, Gardner served as undersecretary of the treasury for Franklin D. Roosevelt. He was also FDR's unofficial advisor and was responsible for many of the ideas presented in the radio Fireside Chats. He died just hours before he was to sail from New York as Harry Truman's ambassador to the Court of St. James.

While governor Gardner led the fight in the 1931 legislature that resulted in the Consolidated University, regarded by many as his greatest political achievement. His will provides an annual award for the faculty member of the sixteen-unit University system "contributing most to the welfare of the human race." One of Gardner's proudest memories was that he served as football captain at both N.C. State while an undergraduate and at UNC while a law student. Gardner-Webb College bears his name in recognition of his benevolences.

Dudley DeWitt Carroll Hall

1953, 1970

A dignified environment in which to train business executives has been created in Carroll Hall, the central building in the School of Business Administration quadrangle. In the new section of Carroll there are special classrooms designed for the M.B.A. program where the case discussion technique is employed instead of the lecture. In addition to the degree programs, there are nearly a dozen courses for executives in such areas as state government, the arts, technical and University management. Notice the imaginative contemporary light bays and the decorative use of one-time exterior walls as corridor surfaces in the new wing. The building was named for Dudley DeWitt Carroll, founder and for thirty years dean of the School of Commerce, and a Kenan professor.

The school took as its objective the development of well-educated businessmen, and Carroll was charged with the responsibility of developing the new division. He demonstrated high intellectual and moral integrity in the teaching of controversial material in the field of social reform.

Carroll received his early education in four-month rural schools and had never been more than seventeen miles from home when he left for Guilford College. His original interest was in classics, but during a postgraduate year at Haverford College he switched to social science and became a practicing economist.

Hanes Hall

1953

Many of the University's permanent records are kept in Hanes Hall, for it contains the offices of both records and registration. It is also headquarters for the Career Planning and Placement Office. The building was named for a prominent Winston-Salem family of industrialists and bankers who, in 1929, established a foundation for the Hanes Collection of Incunabula in the Wilson Library which provided the University with teaching materials not readily obtainable under state funding.

Among the best known of the eight Haneses who established the foundation are:

James Gordon Hanes, chairman of the board of Hanes Hosiery Corporation, whose name is given to an endowed chair in the humanities on the campus and who arranged for the acquisition of UNC's one millionth book in 1960—John Gower's Confessio Amatis, printed by William Caxton in 1483.

Robert M. Hanes, president of the Wachovia Bank and Trust Company and president of the American Bankers Association, who was chief of the mission to Belgium and Luxembourg to administer the Marshall Plan. The Hanes building that houses the Research Triangle Foundation and Institute is named for him.

John W. Hanes, Sr., former undersecretary of the treasury, and an executive of the Olin Corporation.

Dr. Frederick Hanes of the Duke University Medical Faculty, whose name is memorialized in Hanes Hall on that campus.

YMCA

1907

This "crossroads between campus and community" was built when the University abandoned daily compulsory chapel services for all students and deferred religious activities to the YMCA, which had existed on the campus since 1860. In 1935 the YWCA was organized and united with the YMCA. The Campus Police and Traffic Office is also located in the building. Y Court, with its various bulletin boards that are thickly layered with announcements, for many years has been one of the vital communications centers of the campus.

Tens of thousands of student volunteer hours are logged each academic year in dozens of service and educational projects. The Y has always tried to balance personal religious nurture with practical service in the University, a concern for the needy and destitute, and the challenge of current social, religious, and educational concerns.

The first movie in Chapel Hill was screened in the old chapel, and the first juke box was installed there to which the student flappers of the day could dance the Charleston. Thomas Wolfe used an unheated room on the second floor to write in solitude.

Gerrard Hall

1822–37, remodeled 1844, 1879, 1939

Gerrard Hall, the University's second chapel, is the ugly duckling of the campus which architects tried to transform into a swan with Greek Revival adornments in 1844, only to have the trimmings ripped off by a later generation.

The building, used as a small auditorium, has been described as "the plainest of brick structures, with an unattractive hip roof, the eaves barely projecting beyond the walls, plain rectangular windows, and doors at the east front which were mere openings in the wall." A campus information kiosk stands southwest of Gerrard.

Gerrard Hall symbolizes the post-Revolutionary War idea of financing a university with land, often disputed land that won more enemies than the land sales warranted. The land that paid for Gerrard Hall was the gift in 1798 of Major Charles Gerrard. He gave land warrants for 2,560 acres not far from Nashville which he had received for his wartime service and had increased to 13,000 acres by

purchase. Once Gerrard's land had been sold several decades later, the chapel was given his name and construction was completed.

Gerrard was the scene of many important occasions in the University's history. The reopening of the institution after Reconstruction was officially celebrated on 15 September 1875, and portraits of its great men were hung on the walls along with the motto "Laus Deo" wrought in evergreens.

Three presidents of the United States have spoken in Gerrard— Polk and Buchanan while in office and Woodrow Wilson before he became chief executive. Three Cabinet members, including Seward of Seward's Folly (the purchase of Alaska) and a postmaster general, have also been heard there. Andrew Johnson attended commencement in Gerrard while president but did not give a formal address.

For Polk's visit Gerrard was enlarged and the college buildings were repainted. Buchanan, who

Completed in 1837, Gerrard Hall was originally known as New Chapel (courtesy of the North Carolina Collection, the University of North Carolina at Chapel Hill).

was greeted in Chapel Hill by five governors of North Carolina, spoke from the Gerrard platform in 1859 on the need for preserving the Union. While awarding the English prizes, President Buchanan stressed the need of using short sentences, saying that "the ancient style is the best style and that is emphatically the style of Mr. Calhoun and in eminent degree the style of Mr. Webster." He also impressively depicted the evils of drunkenness and urged all to beware of intoxicating liquors.

According to a contemporary report, Gerrard was the scene of Chapel Hill's first musical concert, given by "students and ladies combined, the proceeds going to some religious purpose. . . . The organizer, a beautiful lady, was aided by a violinist, named Mendelssohn from St. Mary's School in Raleigh. In view of the novelty, some predicted rowdyism, but the behavior of the students was excellent and the satisfaction general."

There was no heat in the chapel,

and during the winter there was considerable shivering at public events. "Students usually donned their best clothes for Sunday because ladies were present, but for morning prayers often appeared in shirt and drawers covered by a bed quilt," it has been noted. In Gerrard Hall the applause of foot stamping was allowed but not the pounding of canes.

A panic that could have been dangerous occurred at the commencement of 1846. All seats were filled and many spectators were standing. The galleries of the hall were supported by slender pillars; someone in the audience, probably alarmed by the breaking of a stick outside, shouted, "The gallery is falling." There was a general rush for the doors, and young men had the pleasure of catching young ladies as they jumped from the windows. The president and governor finally calmed the crowd. Before the next commencement additional pillars were installed and the galleries were pronounced safe.

Memorial Hall

1930

More than 170 eminent sons and 5 eminent daughters of Carolina are listed in the hall of fame that lines the lobbies and stairwells of this auditorium, the second building of the same name on the site. The women celebrated on the walls all predate coeducation: four of them were major donors, all named Mary, and the fifth is Cornelia Phillips Spencer, "the lady who rang the bell" when the University reopened after Reconstruction.

The first Memorial Hall, built in 1885, came into being when the governor provided "many thousand bricks from the penitentiary on easy terms." The building was judged not only "architecturally illiterate" but "acoustically perturbing," and President Winston tried to improve the sound by hanging huge muslin draperies from the walls. Largely because of the bad acoustics, it was temporarily converted into a gymnasium in 1895. In 1930 the building was judged unsafe and was razed.

Three of the creators of the mausoleum-like first Memorial Hall, once described as a "foreshortened hexagon like a fat coffin," met with macabre ends. The architect died of sunstroke, and both the assistant architect and the chief mason committed suicide.

Acoustically the second Memorial Hall is excellent and is the scene of major cultural events each season.

Phillips Hall

1918

This English Collegiate building of red tapestry brick with limestone trim houses work in mathematics, statistics, physics/astronomy, and the Computation Center, which is used for research and educational projects by faculty, staff, and students. An IBM 4381 computer is connected to an IBM 3081 in Research Triangle Park, and to a Cyber 205 located at Colorado State University. The campus has a wide variety of decentralized computing services and various departments. A $9.2 million, 73,000-square-foot Computer Science building behind Phillips and Peabody is scheduled for completion in 1986. An interesting collection of Old Weights and Measures may be seen at the ground floor south entrance to the physics section of the building.

The hall is named for three members of the Phillips family whose combined teaching careers at UNC spanned more than sixty years. They were James Phillips, professor of mathematics and natural philosophy, 1826–67; his son Charles Phillips, tutor of mathematics, 1844–54, professor of engineering, 1854–60, professor of mathematics, 1860–68, and again, 1875–79; and his son William Battle Phillips, professor of agricultural chemistry and mining, 1885–88.

Dr. James Phillips was the prime mover in the building of the Chapel Hill Presbyterian Church. He died in Gerrard Hall while presiding at morning chapel services; "the last sounds in his ears were the college bell, the last sight, students assembling for prayer," President Battle wrote.

Peabody Hall

1912, 1960

The School of Education had its roots in the first summer normal school of 1877 although it was not organized as a permanent department until 1885. A new front section was added to the original building in 1960 to harmonize with the Carolina Inn across the street. Inside are specially designed classrooms for demonstration teaching in science and elementary education and an instructional materials center.

This building is the result of the benefactions of George Peabody, even though it was constructed more than a half-century after his death. Peabody was a poor boy from Massachusetts who received four years of schooling, went to work at eleven, carried a salesman's pack throughout the east coast, and finally went to London to establish himself as a dealer in American securities. When he died in England in 1869, he left $3 million to the Southern Education Fund and an identical sum to build apartments in the London slums. Queen Victoria had offered him either a baronetcy or the Grand Cross of the Bath, which he declined, but he did accept the United States Congressional Gold Medal in 1867. After a Westminster Abbey funeral, Peabody's body was returned to America on a new British battleship painted in full mourning and was met at sea by Admiral Farragut. Among Peabody's benefactions were the Peabody Normal College in Nashville and Peabody Institute in Baltimore.

Carolina Inn

1924, 1971

A plaque in the Carolina Inn describes it as "a cheerful inn for visitors, a town hall for the state, and a home for returning sons and daughters of alma mater." The Inn was given to the University in 1935 by its builder, John Sprunt Hill, class of 1889, his wife, and their children. Since enlargement, it provides 145 rooms and suites accommodating 350, and its banquet halls can seat 80 to 450 diners.

The Inn resembles Mount Vernon and is appointed with Oriental rugs, handsome fireplaces, scenic wallpaper, and large mirrors. In the cafeteria is a group of carved wooden circus-parade figures, designed by William Meade Prince, nationally known illustrator, and carved by Carl Boettcher. The Inn is a block from the business district and within an easy walk of most campus points.

Hill was chairman of the University building committee during two great surges in University growth, immediately following each of the World Wars. Under his leadership the century-old size of the University's physical plant was doubled in the 1921–31 decade. He personally gave the University more than a million dollars over a sixty-year period, claiming that it was "the institution of learning that gave me a thousand times more than I can ever repay."

Hill also furnished the original funds for programming the Research Triangle Institute, and he and his wife presented four park and school sites to Durham.

WALK 5

Starting at Brooks Hall;
ending at Mitchell Hall

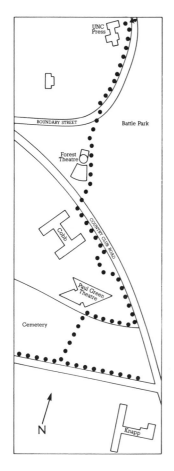

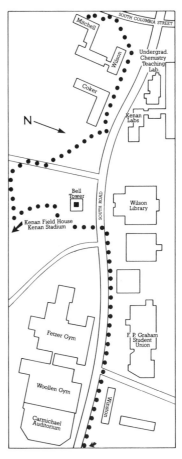

Brooks Hall

1980

The University of North Carolina Press, located in Brooks Hall, was founded in 1922 and is the oldest state university press in the South. It is also one of the oldest in the country. Many of its books have been first of their genre, ranging from *Tobe*, 1939, the first juvenile book for black children which employed photographs of a black family, to *Hiroshima Diary*, 1955, the first book on the Atomic Age to appear in this country. Probably no book from North Carolina has gone out in so many different tongues, for it was translated into a score of languages and forty Swahili dialects. Among the many honors that have come to books published by the Press was a Pulitzer Prize in 1983 for Rhys L. Isaac's *The Transformation of Virginia, 1740–1790*, a pioneering work that treats history from the ground up through reliance on popular records and statistics rather than the pronouncements of political leaders.

The building is named for the family of Aubrey Lee Brooks (1871–1958), who was a benefactor of both the University and the Press. Chief Justice Walter Clark called him "the foremost and most successful lawyer in North Carolina." As solicitor of the Ninth Judicial District, Brooks fought against the tobacco trust and the railroads. He was considered for a seat on the United States Supreme Court by three presidents— Woodrow Wilson, Herbert Hoover, and Franklin D. Roosevelt. At Chapel Hill, Brooks set up the Brooks Scholarship Fund of more than $1 million and established the first endowment for the Press. The Press published four of his books, and he received a Chapel Hill honorary degree.

Battle Park

1924

A handsome 100-acre wedge of venerable woodland beginning near the center of the campus coincides with much of the original 125-acre land grant made to the University in 1792 and 1796 by Hardy Morgan. The forest was diminished by sale over the years, especially during bankruptcy proceedings against the University in 1881.

Some of these tracts were returned to the University by three gifts of the Junior Order of Gimghouls, a social group of students, alumni, and faculty, founded in 1889, whose medieval-style castle, built by Waldensian stone masons, adjoins the park on the southeast. The gifts were designated for park use. The University now owns about 66 acres of the forest, and the town of Chapel Hill owns the rest.

The forest commemorates the creative and recreative spirit of President Kemp P. Battle, called the "Southern Thoreau," who cleared paths and built benches and bridges in the forest (see Senlac). He gave fanciful names to his favorite haunts, such as Dogwood Dingle, Trysting Poplar, and Flirtation Knoll. Near Gimghoul Castle, a semicircular seat at Piney Prospect overlook bears a plaque to "Kemp Plummer Battle, 1831–1919, who knew and loved these woods as no one else."

Several trees in Battle Park have been transformed by art students into whimsical sculpture. Along the path next to the creek may be seen (about 100 feet northeast of the Forest Theatre at the right) a stump transformed into a witch; at the first footbridge, at right, a totem pole of cans; and at the third footbridge, at left, a small carved raccoon peering from a hole in a tree, his paw raised in solemn greeting.

Forest Theatre

1919

Outdoor drama was first performed in Battle Park in 1916 to celebrate the tercentenary of Shakespeare's death. W. C. Coker, faculty botanist who had developed the Arboretum nearby, chose the location. Several years later, when "Proff" Frederick Koch came to the campus (after having built a unique outdoor theater at the University of North Dakota, the first to use a stream between stage and audience), the Battle Park location was developed into a permanent theater.

The theater was rebuilt with WPA funds about 1940 to a plan of Albert Q. Bell, who designed outdoor theaters for historic dramas at Manteo, Cherokee, and Williamsburg, Virginia. In 1948 it was improved to a plan by architect Paul Beidler.

The Forest Theatre is dedicated to "Proff" Koch, the founder of the original Carolina Playmakers and the father of folk drama in America. The inscription on the dedicatory marker at the entrance to the theater reads: "For here now under the greenwood tree in a new-world forest of Arden, through love and admiration of thousands of students, is dedicated . . . this open air palace of light and sound, haunt of birds and breezes and human voices, home of natural beauty, poetry and drama, set upon the warm earth, in enduring stone, to commemorate an ardent genius who inspired and fostered the American folk play and, like another Johnny Appleseed, sowed the creative seeds of communal authorship throughout the American continent."

The theater is frequently used for weddings, outdoor concerts, and other events.

Paul Green Theatre

1978

Designed in the form of two triangles joined by a hallway–work area, the Paul Green Theatre, planned by A. B. Odell Associates of Charlotte, is an action theater with a thrust stage that can be raised or lowered in sections. The auditorium, which seats 500, was named for the creator of the outdoor symphonic drama form, winner of a 1927 Pulitzer Prize for *In Abraham's Bosom*, and author of more than sixty dramas which won him the reputation of North Carolina's finest regional playwright. Green also taught philosophy at the University.

Much of Paul Green's writing stemmed from the campus and the original Carolina Playmakers, although he spent a number of years in Hollywood, where his twenty film scripts included State Fair. *Will Rogers played in a number of Green's scripts.*

Green's first play, Surrender to the Enemy, *was based on the well-known Chapel Hill story of the romance between the Yankee general occupying the village after the Civil War and the daughter of President David Swain. The play, written when Green was a twenty-two-year-old freshman, was produced in the spring of 1917 on the hillside where the Forest Theatre is now located.*

The Lost Colony, the first of Paul Green's symphonic dramas, opened in 1937 at the Waterside Theater in Manteo, with President Franklin D. Roosevelt in the audience. The play was produced to commemorate the 350th anniversary of Sir Walter Raleigh's first attempt to colonize the New World, and has been performed each summer except the years of World War II, when the coast was blacked out against Nazi submarines. The historic drama movement which Green began at Manteo became nationwide, extending all the way to Kodiak, Alaska. Green himself wrote sixteen symphonic dramas.

Old Chapel Hill Cemetery

c. 1798

JANE TENNEY
GILBERT
I WAS A TAR HEEL BORN
AND A TAR HEEL BRED
AND HERE I LIE
A TAR HEEL DEAD
BORN JAN. 2, 1896
AND STILL HERE 1980

The earliest gravestone in the Old Chapel Hill Cemetery bears the date 1798; it is that of student George Clarke, who died at age nineteen. The grave is found outside the east edge of the fenced Dialectic Society plot near the center of the burial ground. There are unmarked graves, probably earlier, in the section closest to Alexander, Connor, and Winston dormitories, where slaves were buried.

The 6.5-acre Chapel Hill Cemetery describes, through its headstones, the special quality of a university town—the luminous life of the mind as it has been lived in the place for nineteen decades. Graves of early students reflect an era when it was not possible to take bodies home for interment. They are buried in the two iron-fenced plots established by the Dialectic and Philanthropic literary societies, who were not only artists in the epitaph but often furnished the headstones for their comrades.

The graves of four university presidents are located in the cemetery: Francis Preston Venable, eighth president, from 1900–1914; Edward Kidder Graham, ninth president, from 1914–1918; his successor, Acting President Marvin H. Stacy, who, like Graham, died in the influenza epidemic of World War I; and Frank Porter Graham, who first was president of the Chapel Hill campus and then president of the Consolidated University. The epitaph of Dr. and Mrs. Graham reads: "They had faith in youth, and youth responded with their best."

A recent tombstone that attracts many visitors is found just inside the stone fence at the drive across from the east end of the tennis courts, which reads: "I was a Tar Heel born / and a Tar Heel bred / and here I lie / a Tar Heel dead."

Institute of Government (Knapp Building)

1956

For more than fifty years, since its founding in 1931, the Institute of Government has helped public employees and officials perform the task of governing and has increased public understanding of state and local government. It is the largest and most diversified governmental training and research organization in the United States. Sam Ervin, speaking on the floor of the Senate, called it "the first facility of its kind in the history of the world."

The neocolonial-style Knapp Building was named for Joseph Palmer Knapp, publisher of a number of national magazines, who owned a vacation home in Currituck County and did much to benefit that area. Pictures from the Knapp family collection are on display in the building and the auditorium has a group of murals depicting events and individuals notable in North Carolina history.

The Institute of Government was founded and directed for thirty

years by Albert Coates. A double portrait, done by Sarah Blakeslee Speight, of Coates and his wife Gladys is found in the entry hall. The soft, informal scene shows the Coateses with the porch of their house in the background—a particularly significant scenic choice. Coates financed the early years of the institute at his own expense; for three years it was necessary for the couple to give up their home and live in a rented room.

In recent years the Institute of Government has reached 20,000 persons per year through short courses on the campus and elsewhere in the state. Since 1935 it has furnished a Legislative Reporting Service that provides the only complete, published source of information on the work of the General Assembly on a day-to-day basis. During the 1984 short session of the legislature, it reported on 120,000 items.

William Donald Carmichael Auditorium

1965

Woollen Gymnasium

1937

This is one of three buildings in the University system named for William D. Carmichael, Jr. (others are at North Carolina State University and UNC-Greensboro), who left a New York career as advertising executive and broker to work with the three units of the University then involved in consolidation. He was a prodigious fundraiser for each campus, and was fond of saying, "I'll take the cash and let the credit go." Chapel Hill basketball teams became national powers in this building under the coaching of Dean Smith. Students who played here included gold medal members of the 1976 Olympics at Montreal coached by Dean Smith—Phil Ford, Walter Davis, Tom LaGarde, and Mitch Kupchak—as well as 1984 Los Angeles Olympic stars Michael Jordan and Sam Perkins.

Charles T. Woollen, for whom this building was named, was a major figure in University administration between 1901 and 1938. The Bowman Gray Memorial Pool was given in memory of the principal executive of the R. J. Reynolds Tobacco Company, who died in 1938 on the steamship *Kungsholm* off the North Cape and was buried at sea according to his wish.

Robert Allison Fetzer Gymnasium

1981

Winner of a national design prize, this building was named for Chapel Hill's first director of physical education and athletics (1923–52) who began the expansion that brought national renown to the Tar Heel athletic program. As head track coach, he turned out scores of individual conference champions, three national champions, and two Olympic competitors. The building contains three gymnasiums, six squash courts, and fifteen handball and racketball courts.

Morehead-Patterson Memorial Tower

1930

The ten-bell carillon of the Morehead-Patterson Tower first rang in November 1931 to lead University students to "bear high the torch of progress and to do their part for the betterment of humanity." Designed by McKim, Mead, and White, the tower is 172 feet tall, but since it is set on a knoll its actual rise is about 200 feet. Visible for several miles, it is also occasionally audible as far as Durham. The tower was the $100,000 gift of John Motley Morehead III, class of 1891, and Rufus Lenoir Patterson, class of 1893, honoring members of their families who had been associated with the University throughout its entire history. At present, sixteen Moreheads and eleven Pattersons are commemorated on the tablets beneath the arcade.

The largest bell, which tolls the hours, is engraved with the name of Governor John Motley Morehead, onetime president of the Alumni Association, and the next largest is inscribed to Revolutionary General William Lenoir, first chairman of the UNC Board of Trustees.

Originally rung manually, the carillon now operates electronically to call students to classes, provide twilight music, and serenade the dispersing crowd after football games. Among the tunes played at the dedication was the old Scotch-Presbyterian hymn, "How Tedious and Tasteless the Hours When Jesus I No Longer See," the favorite of donor Morehead's grandmother, who sang ten children to sleep with it.

Kenan Memorial Stadium

1928, 1963

Kenan Stadium, given as a memorial to his parents by William Rand Kenan, Jr., originally contained 25,000 seats, but in 1963 was enlarged to 43,000. Kenan was deeply interested in the athletic program of his alma mater.

The football games that take place here on fall Saturday afternoons are a strong unifying element for hundreds of thousands of friends of the University. Fans come from all over the state with tail-gate picnics. The plan for parking cars begins early in the morning on the day of a game when dozens of attendants fan out over the campus with orange traffic cones. Half-times are enlivened by the Tar Heel marching band, the appearance of the mascot Rameses the Ram, who has blessed the proceedings for more than 60 years (there have been 14 Rameses to date, each with white wool cleaned and curried, curled horns painted Tar Heel blue), and a highly skilled cheerleading squad. Librarian Louis Round Wilson, writing in the one-hundredth year of his life, recalled Kenan Stadium as an "exquisite natural-architectural creation," in which visitors enjoy the sight of the "green-carpeted" football field and the "brilliance of the display of the yellow of the poplars and hickories, the red and russet of the oaks, intermingled with the green of the pines."

Near the Kenan Field House, a Student Athletic Development Center is expected to be completed in January 1987. It will contain study and conference rooms, typing and video laboratories, and areas for academic counseling for University athletes.

William C. Coker Hall

1963

Named for botanist William Chambers Coker, a Kenan professor and faculty member from 1902 to 1945 (see Arboretum), the building contains a herbarium which Coker founded in 1903. Within the last decade, it has come to be ranked third among university collections and tied for fifth (with the Smithsonian Institution) among all herbaria in the nation. More than 600,000 specimens are in the collection; some of them are the most complete or representative of their respective plant groups in the world.

Wilson Hall

1940, addition 1965

Headquarters for the Department of Biology, this building was named for Henry Van Peters ("Froggie") Wilson, whose forty-seven-year career at the University between 1891 and 1939 began as head of a one-man department where he frugally doled out corks and vials for laboratory work. He was among the first five Kenan professors to be appointed. In 1902 Wilson established at Beaufort, N.C., the first permanent marine biological laboratory south of New England. He originated a new field of experimental research, a new way of studying the behavior of living cells, and did much work with sponges. The building's ground floor lobby contains specimens of birds, eggs, nests, animals, butterflies, insects, fossils, corals, and shells.

Elisha Mitchell Hall

1964

The historic role played by Elisha Mitchell, faculty member from 1818 to 1857, in the early life of the University is noted in the introduction to this guide. He participated in the work of the first state geological survey in the nation, which had been begun between 1822 and 1826 by Dennison Olmsted. The Elisha Mitchell Scientific Society, founded in 1883, was the first such learned society in the South. Its journal has exchanged scholarly material with institutions in all parts of the globe.

WALK 6

Starting at Beard Hall;
ending at North
Carolina Memorial
Hospital

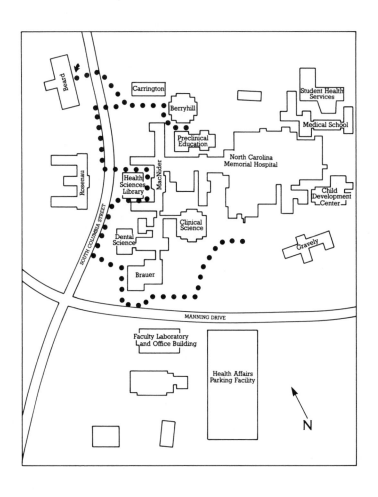

Beard Hall

1959

The School of Pharmacy building is named for its second dean, John Grover Beard, who, during 1931–40, made annual visits to every member of the North Carolina Pharmaceutical Association and served as a major officer in three national organizations. Over the building's front door are decorative urns that suggest the shape of apothecary jars. Inside is a museum collection of pharmacy equipment of yesteryear, and in the library are some unusual apothecary jars, including one dating to the seventeenth century.

Carrington Hall

1969

A contemporary School of Nursing building of brick and concrete rising from a large deck is named for Elizabeth Scott Carrington, an extraordinary public servant who improved the quality of nursing education in North Carolina and the nation. Mrs. Carrington helped persuade James N. Johnston to earmark a sizable part of his major scholarship bequest to the University for nursing students at various levels.

Berryhill Hall (Basic Medical Sciences)

1970

An eight-story contemporary red brick teaching laboratory for basic medical sciences is located between Carrington Hall and an older red brick Medical Sciences Research Building (1962). It was named in 1973 to honor Dr. W. Reece Berryhill, a faculty member for thirty years, a Sarah Graham Kenan Professor, and Dean of the School of Medicine from 1941 to 1964, who made a sixty-year-old dream of a four-year medical school at Chapel Hill into a reality. The School of Medicine had been established as a two-year course in 1879.

Dr. Berryhill defined the need for a state-supported medical school in North Carolina, enlisted legislative support for the project, planned the school's development, and recruited the clinical faculty. When he retired in 1964, he worked with

a number of the state's community hospitals to build the base for the North Carolina Area Health Education Center program. This program, founded in 1972, was an award-winning prototype for subsequent AHECs in other states.

Dr. Berryhill was a model of personal integrity. One day when he had driven to work in a state car for an official errand late in the day, he was told of an emergency at home. He ran to a colleague and asked, "May I borrow your car? My barn is burning and I shouldn't drive a state car there."

Notorious for his illegible physician's handwriting, Dr. Berryhill once scribbled something indecipherable on a student's examination paper. With trepidation the student asked the dean to translate. The message read: "Your handwriting is so terrible I don't see how you can ever get through medical school."

Brinkhous-Bullitt Preclinical Education Building

1973

A concrete contemporary high-rise south of Berryhill Hall houses work in pathology and facilities for the state medical examiner. The building is named for Dr. Kenneth M. Brinkhous (faculty member, 1946–80), a world-renowned researcher in hemostasis, thrombosis, and blood products, and Dr. James B. Bullitt (faculty member in pathology from 1913 to 1947), who was particularly interested in hookworm, trichinosis, tuberculosis, and neoplasia. He often remarked that, during his early years in Chapel Hill, when two pathologists met, they constituted a quorum for a meeting of the North Carolina Society of Pathology. Dr. Bullitt was well informed in prehistory and gathered a significant group of paleolithic artifacts.

Rosenau Hall

1962

Health Sciences Library

1970

Back on Pittsboro Road, the neo-classic red brick School of Public Health building commemorates its first dean, Milton J. Rosenau, internationally known as the "Father of Public Health" and by some as the "Father of Preventive Medicine." He founded the School of Public Health in 1936 after retiring from Harvard. There he had begun the nation's first school for health officers in 1913. Dr. Rosenau's creed was, "The first duty of government is to protect the health of its citizens, for without health and vigor nations perish." Today, the school consistently ranks in the top half-dozen in the nation. In the first floor public spaces is a small collection of contemporary paintings and sculpture—purchase-prize acquisitions from art shows held at the school for a number of years.

Originally a three-story building that was increased to six levels in the late 1970s, the Health Sciences Library in 1984 ranked seventh among the largest and most active medical facilities in the United States and Canada. It is the largest in the South. A Rare Book room is open to serious scholars of health history.

MacNider Hall

1939

The present Health Sciences complex began in this building (entered through a neoclassic portico behind the Health Sciences Library). At the outset, it contained all the teaching units that have grown into separate schools and departments. The building is named for Dr. William deB. MacNider, dean of the School of Medicine from 1937 to 1940, a Kenan professor, and a faculty member for more than half a century. Dr. MacNider enjoyed national recognition as a scientist and investigator in renal physiology and pathology.

MacNider Hall contains the administrative offices of the School of Medicine, although the work extends to a complex of buildings around it. The University is one of the few in the nation with a full range of professional health schools on the same campus. More than 3,000 students are enrolled in the five health disciplines.

The School of Medicine has a wide reputation as a teaching institution and research center. In recent years it has attracted more than $40 million annually in federal research grants, third-ranked in the nation for grant approval rate. Much emphasis has been placed on cancer research, and in 1984 a new Lineberger Cancer Research Center was dedicated west of the parking deck. The center honors a family of Belmont industrialists. The Program for International Training in Health has instructed more than 28,000 persons in Africa and the Middle East during its first five years.

Brauer Hall (Dental Education Building)

1969

Dr. John C. Brauer played an important part in planning the present three-building dental complex, of which this is the nerve center. He was the first dean of the School of Dentistry, from 1950 to 1966, and was considered to be the best-qualified dental educator in the United States when he arrived from the University of Southern California to begin his task of working with forty students in two World War II quonsets. In 1966, when he retired, the school had become one of the top five in the nation, and in 1973 ranked number one.

Dr. Brauer was a pioneer in children's dentistry, was president and co-founder of the American Academy of Pedodontics, and president of the American Society of Dentistry for Children.

On the second floor of Brauer Hall is a collection of art objects including a marble sculpture by Rodin, *The Hand of God*.

Burnett-Womack Clinical Sciences Building

1975

Burnett-Womack, east of the School of Dentistry, is a clinical sciences building for medicine, surgery, pediatrics, dermatology, ophthalmology, neurology, and anesthesiology. It is named for Charles H. Burnett, first chairman of the Department of Medicine between 1951 and 1964, and Dr. Nathan A. Womack, first chairman of the Department of Surgery between 1951 and 1975 and a Kenan professor. The Womack Surgical Society was founded in honor of the latter in 1968. Both men created departments that were widely recognized for their excellence.

North Carolina Memorial Hospital

1952

North Carolina Memorial Hospital, a referral and teaching hospital of more than 600 beds, is a national leader in dealing with arthritis, autism, burns, cancer, coagulation disorders, infectious diseases, infertility, and neuromuscular diseases. The hospital is also a center for the care of high-risk mothers and infants. The first "test tube baby" in North Carolina and test tube triplets came from the hospital.

The complex of buildings includes a gift shop, eating places, motel, and the John M. Reeves All Faiths Chapel. The chapel focuses on a sculpture done by Clark Fitz-Gerald representing an opening milkweed pod, its seeds being scattered in the wind. The sculpture symbolizes the basic theological principles of hope and regeneration. Hospitalized persons attend chapel in person or can take part via television in their rooms. The hospital conducts a school for youngsters between five and nineteen, generally enrolling about fifty.

The Student Health Center (1980), part of the medical complex but adjacent to Kenan Stadium, is one of the most comprehensive student services in the nation.

Several sections of the hospital bear names of North Carolina business and civic leaders, including the patient-receiving area, named for J. Spencer Love, Burlington Industries manufacturer, and the new critical care wing, named for Esley O. Anderson, Jr., Charlotte businessman and long-time chairman of the hospital's board. Gravely Building, originally a tuberculosis sanitarium, was named for L. L. Gravely of Rocky Mount, a state legislator who worked for tuberculosis care. Several members of his family suffered from the disease.

More than 20,000 patients are admitted to the hospital each year and visits to the hospital's 160 clinics total nearly 300,000.

The last three subjects in this guide are a distance from the central campus and have parking space for visits by car.

Student Activities Center

1985

The $33.8 million Student Activities Center will be the home floor for the Tar Heel basketball team beginning with the 1985–86 season. Beneath a 115-foot, diamond-shaped translucent dome admitting natural light is a 21,600-seat arena.

The center includes a 10-lane, 50-meter swimming pool which will allow such events as NCAA championships and Olympic trials. The building also contains a memorabilia room, a donors room, and athletic offices.

William Rand Kenan, Jr., Center of North Carolina

1986

The activities of the Kenan Fund and the Kenan Institute, established to support the study of private enterprise, will be housed in this center. The five-story, 60,000-square foot building will also provide meeting, seminar, research, and study facilities for many University-related activities.

The Kenan family surname has been involved with higher education in North Carolina since 1790. William Rand Kenan, Jr.'s, paternal great-great-grandfather, James Kenan, was on the University's first board of trustees; his maternal great-great-grandfather, Christopher Barbee, donated 221 acres, or about one-fifth of the campus of that day. Several members of the family's sixth generation have established four categories of endowed professorships. The earliest of the chairs, established in 1917 and known simply as the Kenan Professors, exist only at Chapel Hill; they number twenty-three. The first of the William Rand Kenan, Jr., Professorships, established in 1965, which now number eighty-six at more than fifty institutions throughout the United States, were awarded on the Chapel Hill campus. Two Graham Kenan Professorships in Law and four Sarah Graham Kenan Professorships in Medicine were established in 1962.

North Carolina
Botanical Garden

1952

More than 30,000 visitors to the North Carolina Botanical Garden each year are invited "to walk the trail at different seasons, to enjoy the changing variety in nature." Three miles of interpretive trails wind through the garden's 307 acres. One of the outstanding native plant gardens in the nation, the North Carolina Botanical Garden is a regional center for research, conservation, and interpretation of southeastern flora.

The garden's walking trails follow the contours of the rolling piedmont hillsides covered by pines, oaks, and hickories. Morgan Creek runs through the garden. Special habitats display the distinctive vegetation of the coastal plain, the mountains, and the sandhills. Greenhouses contain rare insectivorous plants—pitcher plants, trumpets, butterworts, sundew, and Venus' flytrap, which grows in its natural state only within a seventy-five-mile radius of Wilmington, N.C. Mountain plants found on the garden's hardwood-covered north slopes include Canadian hemlock, a number of species of rhododendron and azaleas, mountain laurel, galax, cranberries, and the rare shortia. In the sandhills habitat is the distinctive longleaf pine of that region. A comprehensive herb garden is also cultivated.

The Totten Center, 1976, houses the interpretive, administrative, and maintenance services of the garden. The building commemorates Dr. Henry Roland Totten, for fifty years professor of Botany, and his wife Addie Williams Totten, "Mrs. Garden Club of North Carolina." The couple died three weeks apart in 1974. Dr. Totten helped develop the Arboretum, and was co-author, with W. C. Coker, of *Trees of North Carolina* and *Trees of the Southeastern States*. The center is landscaped in trees, shrubs, vines, and flowers of particular significance to the Tottens, including a Totten's Oak, a hybrid named for Dr. Totten.